The ASTON VILLA MISCELLANY

The ASTON VILLA MISCELLANY

By DAVE WOODHALL

VSP

Vision Sports Publishing
19–23 High Street
Kingston on Thames
Surrey
KT1 1LL

www.visionsp.co.uk

Published by Vision Sports Publishing in 2012

ISBN 13: 978-1-907637-73-5

Printed and bound in China by
Toppan Printing Co Ltd

Typeset in Sabon MT by Palimpsest Book Production Limited,
Falkirk, Stirlingshire

A CIP catalogue record for this book is
available from the British Library

Acknowledgements

First of all, thanks to Jim Drewett for giving me what proved to be an enthralling and thoroughly enjoyable commission. Even after so many years supporting and writing about the Villa I was able to learn more about our club due to his encouragement.

Thanks also to those who have helped fill gaps both in my knowledge and my source material – Greg Upton, Simon Inglis, Peter Page, Mac McColgan, Rob Bishop, John Russell and Geoff Coleman, plus anyone else I've inadvertently left out. Jörn Mårtensson's online Aston Villa Player Database has also been a great help. And also, a big thank you to the staff at the Birmingham Central Library for continuing to keep their local newspaper archives in immaculate condition.

Finally I'd like to apologise to everyone (and one lady in particular) I've kept awake over the past six months by endlessly repeating facts, figures and stories I've unearthed. It won't happen again. Much.

Author's note: All the stats in the *Aston Villa Miscellany* are correct up to the start of the 2012/13 season.

Foreword

In the summer of 1979 I joined Aston Villa, and although I later played all over the world my heart has always remained at Villa Park. I'd known Villa were a famous club with an enviable history when I signed for them, although like most new arrivals it wasn't until I actually came to Birmingham that I realised just how big they were. Villa Park and the training ground at Bodymoor Heath were different to anything I'd ever been used to before. The expectation levels from supporters and the interest the local press showed were frightening.

My new manager, Ron Saunders, promised me that we were going to do well, and believe me, you wouldn't argue with the boss when he told you what he was going to do. But even so, I never imagined the success we would enjoy as part of the great team he put together. First, of course, we were league champions in 1980/81 and I also won the Goal of the Season award for that one against Everton. Then we won the European Cup the following year, and not only did I score a couple of decent goals on the way to the final, I was also involved in the build-up to Peter Withe's winner against Bayern Munich – I shared an assist with the post. And then there was the European Super Cup win against Barcelona, which was equally memorable in its own way. Three players sent off, Gordon Cowans kicked into the back of the net, and it hardly made the headlines the following day. A story like that would be international news for weeks nowadays.

After leaving Villa I travelled around the world playing football, and wherever I went the name Aston Villa meant something. It seemed that everyone wanted to talk about them and ask me what it was like to have played for the Villa. Maybe it was only then, when I was so far away, that I realised just what a magical club it is, and one that I have been proud to be associated with. When I retired from playing I returned to live in the area, and I was able to watch the Villa more regularly. I've always been made welcome at the ground, my friends say Villa Park is the best place in the country to watch football and that's not just because there's a permanent reminder of the club's – and my – finest hour emblazoned across the North Stand. As the banner says, "*There's a good ball played in for Tony Morley.*" I'll remember those words as long as I live.

One of the many reasons why I feel Villa are so special is the people associated with the club. From Randy Lerner down, they all share a feeling of togetherness and a love of Aston Villa. And once you've been a part of that special bond, it never leaves you. The saying "Once a Villa man, always a Villa man" is absolutely true. Whenever I attend functions with the Former Players Association or turn out for the Old Stars in charity games, the feeling that we're all part of one big claret and blue family is still there, and will always remain.

Reading through this book has reminded me of many of the good times I had as a player, and also some of the more recent ones I've witnessed as a supporter. It's reminded me about some of the people I've known, whether they be famous players, managers or the unsung heroes behind the scenes, and told me a lot about the history of the Villa that I didn't know. Did Villa really have a winger who played under an umbrella when it was raining? I'd like to have seen Ron Saunders' face if I'd tried to do that. I could believe him emulating an earlier Villa official and kidnapping a player who was about to sign for another team, though.

These are just a couple of the stories that have reinforced my belief that Aston Villa are more than just a football club, and that to have played for them is indeed a great honour. I'm sure there will be many more tales to be recorded in the club's future. It's a fascinating book. I've enjoyed reading it and I hope you do, too.

Tony Morley

— VILLA'S FORMATION —

"This new fangled football thing looks like fun!"

As with many great tales, the story of Villa's formation is shrouded in mystery. It's a matter of legend that a group of young men, members of the Aston Villa Wesleyan Church cricket team, met under a lamp-post in Heathfield Road, part of what is now the Birmingham suburb of Lozells, during 1874 and talked about the formation of a football team in order to keep fit during the winter, after watching an impromptu game in a nearby field. Members of the team present included William Scattergood, Jack Hughes, Frederick Matthews and Walter Price, with Hughes being elected captain.

It has long been claimed that Villa's first official game was against local rugby team Aston Brook St Mary's, and took place at Wilson Road, Birchfield. The first half, played under rugby rules, ended goalless. With the second half being given over to the then-prevalent Association (Sheffield) code, Villa secured their first-ever win thanks to a goal scored by Jack Hughes, with a ball hired for 1/6d for the afternoon. The *Birmingham Morning News* report on March 16th 1875 of such a game almost certainly refers to this event.

However, in January of that year, an 'Aston Villa' team was recorded as having taken part in two football matches against the newly-formed Aston Park Unity FC, an offshoot of Aston Unity cricket club, in Aston Park. These were regarded as full club matches by Unity, although the Villa side has been described as a scratch team drawn from members of the Aston Villa cricket club. Whatever the truth behind these games, there appears to be an anomaly in the club's history. Either Aston Villa FC were founded prior to January 1875, in which case their first match was against Aston Park Unity, rather than as has always been thought, Aston Brook St Mary's, or the commonly-accepted formation date of 1874 is wrong, and the club didn't come into existence until at the earliest February of the following year.

— LOCAL RIVALS —

Villa's rivalry with West Bromwich Albion is the oldest in world football, dating back well before the formation of the Football League in 1888. Of all the games between the clubs, none was a greater disappointment for the Villa than the clash at the Hawthorns on April 29th 1959. Villa needed to win to make sure of avoiding relegation from the old First Division, and were 1–0 up until late on. However, Ronnie Allen equalised to send them down on goal average and save Manchester City, who beat Leicester 3–1 in a game that kicked off 15 minutes later than did proceedings at the Hawthorns.

Villa manager Joe Mercer, who of course went on to great success as City manager in the 1960s, knew nothing of this late twist as he had left the ground – with his side still in the lead – to attend a dinner in honour of Wolves and England captain Billy Wright. Mercer arrived at the venue for the dinner, the Midland Hotel in Birmingham, completely unaware of the dramatic finale to the season and was visibly shocked to be told upon his arrival that his club had been relegated. He had previously managed Sheffield United to relegation, and when arriving at Villa Park the following day, he was met with a telegram from a United supporter that read, "Congratulations Mercer. You've done it again."

Many years later Allen, by now suffering from the first stages of Alzheimer's disease, was granted a testimonial by the Albion. To show there was no ill-feeling, Villa happily agreed to provide the opposition and a crowd of 14,000 provided healthy receipts of £80,000 to help the player during his last days.

— THE FIRST GLORY —

The first of many!

By the mid 1880s Villa were beginning to create a national name for themselves and looking to have an impact on the FA Cup when the 1886/87 competition got underway. Their first round opponents were Wednesbury Old Athletic, one of the early pioneers of Midlands football but by then a shadow of their former selves. A 13–0 scoreline in this game remains the Villa's record victory.

Derby Midland were brushed aside 6–1 in the second round, but Villa's next opponents were to provide a much stiffer test. Wolverhampton Wanderers were also coming to the forefront of local football, and held Villa to a 2–2 draw at Wellington Road on December 11th 1886. Wolves' Dudley Road ground saw an epic replay finish 1–1 after extra-time and the FA insisted that Wolves would also have home advantage for the second replay, which finished with the sides sharing six goals. Finally, on January 29th 1887, seven weeks after their initial contest, a crowd of 12,000 packed into Wellington Road in gale-force winds to witness Villa win 2–0.

Villa were given a bye in the fourth round, then came a routine 5–0 victory over Linconshire side Horncastle before facing the formidable Lancastrians, Darwen, in the sixth round, at Perry Barr.

The story goes that Villa, 3–0 up, were visited in their dressing room at half-time by the President of Moseley Rugby Club and he handed round a loving cup filled with champagne to the players. Needless to say, they accepted and, equally obviously, were scarcely in any fit state to see out a second half in which Darwen pulled back two goals and were unlucky not to win.

In the semi-final Villa were drawn to play against Rangers – this being the last season that Scottish clubs were permitted to enter the FA Cup. The game took place at Crewe – presumably because the Cheshire railway town offered convenient transport links for the Glaswegian side. Villa won what was at that time the biggest victory in their history, beating what was virtually a Scottish international select by three goals to one.

Villa's opponents in the final were West Bromwich Albion, runners-up the previous year and such strong favourites that they had already planned to bring back the cup to their home town by train via South Wales to prevent it travelling through Birmingham. But the trophy was to take the direct route to Aston, as Villa won the game, played at Kennington Oval before a crowd of 20,000, by two goals to nil, the scorers being Dennis Hodgetts and captain Archie Hunter.

— CHAMPIONS I: 1893/94 —

Villa's golden age began with this, their first league championship, notable for 84 goals from just 30 games. They finished six points clear of Sunderland's 'team of all the talents,' who had won the title the previous two years and would win it again the following season.

	P	W	D	L	F	A	Pts
Aston Villa	**30**	**19**	**6**	**5**	**84**	**42**	**44**
Sunderland	30	17	4	9	72	44	38
Derby County	30	16	4	10	73	62	36
Blackburn Rovers	30	16	2	12	69	53	34
Burnley	30	15	4	11	61	51	34
Everton	30	15	3	12	90	57	33
Nottingham Forest	30	14	4	12	57	48	32
West Bromwich Albion	30	14	4	12	66	59	32
Wolverhampton Wanderers	30	14	3	13	52	63	31
Sheffield United	30	13	5	12	47	61	31
Stoke	30	13	3	14	65	79	29
Sheffield Wednesday	30	9	8	13	48	57	26
Bolton Wanderers	30	10	4	16	38	52	24
Preston North End	30	10	3	17	44	56	23
Darwen	30	7	5	18	37	83	19
Newton Heath	30	6	2	22	36	72	14

— THE HISTORY OF ASTON —

In 1066, Aston (then known as Estone, meaning the east village or estate, although the place it was east of is unknown) was one of the many manors held by Earl Edwin, who was allowed to keep his lands after the Norman Conquests, until fleeing the country five years later following a failed Anglo-Saxon rebellion. The Domesday Book of 1086 recorded that the manor of Estone was held by Godmund, a Saxon, from William FitzAnsculf, a great lord based at Dudley, who also controlled much of what is now north Birmingham. Aston had a church, a mill, a wood three miles long and half a mile broad, and eight hides. The population was made up of '30 villeins', 'twelve bordars' and 'one serf', plus their families. The manor itself was worth 100 shillings and had a population of about 200, making it five times the size of Birmingham.

During the 13th and early 14th centuries Aston Manor, then part of the county of Warwickshire, passed to the de Erdingtons and then the Grimsarwes, the male line of which died out during the 15th century. The heiress of the family, Maude, married a wool merchant, John atte Holte, Aston Manor passing to their son and staying in the hands of the Holtes for some 400 years.

The Holtes did well out of the dissolution of the monastries during the time of Henry VIII. Thomas Holte, a lawyer, acted as local commissioner for the dissolution, and was able to buy much of the land that had belonged to religious houses, thereby establishing the family as one of the wealthiest in the area. Their lands included much of what later became part of Birmingham and Solihull, stretching as far away as Deritend, to the south of what is now the city centre, and Water Orton, eight miles to the east of Aston. With the family's fortunes rising, Thomas's grandson, also named Thomas (see *The First Holte Ender*, page 44), built Aston Hall during the early part of the 17th century.

However, during the late 18th century, the lack of a male heir led to the great estates created by the Holtes going out of the direct family, and into the hands of distant relatives. Poor business investments soon led to these lands having to be divided and sold, transforming amongst other areas the village of Aston Manor from a small rural village in 1848 to a thriving community with a population of 54,000 by the early 1890s. By this time the expansion of first the canal and then the rail networks had placed Aston firmly in the heart of the industrial Midlands, and such notable businesses as Ansell's brewery, the HP sauce factory and the Norton motorcycle works helped fuel the area's growth. The impressive church of St Peter & St Paul, dating back to the fifteenth century, was rebuilt between 1879–90.

In 1869, Aston Manor was governed by the Aston Manor Local Board, in 1884 the district was granted its own Member of Parliament and in 1903 it was incorporated as a separate borough. Finally, in 1911 Aston Manor lost its independence and became part of Birmingham. Apart from the great historical buildings of church, hall and football ground, little remains of the old Aston.

— THE VIKING —

Olof Mellberg: The Viking

Olof Mellberg was signed from Racing Santander in the summer of 2001. He immediately became a favourite with Villa supporters and over the next seven years turned in a series of impressive displays, both in his favoured central defensive position and also at right-back. He was Villa captain for some years and also captained Sweden, for whom he won 107 caps. Olof's cult hero status was cemented in 2002, when he said, "I don't like Birmingham City at all." He also created a piece of history when becoming the first player to score at Arsenal's new Emirates Stadium, during a 1–1 draw in August 2006. In January 2008 Mellberg announced that he had signed a pre-contract with Juventus, and it was tribute to his standing amongst Villa supporters that this news brought no criticism of the player, but instead an appreciation of his abilities. The final games of

Mellberg's Villa career took on the air of a farewell tour. He was substituted during the dying moments of Villa's 5–1 win over Birmingham City, enabling him to receive a standing ovation from the crowd, then the final home game of the season, against Wigan, was designated 'Olof Mellberg Day' with Villa supporters wearing Viking outfits and waving Swedish flags. The following week, Mellberg's last game for the club, away at West Ham, saw him buying replica shirts for all 3,000 traveling supporters. The shirts, with Mellberg's name and 'THANKS 4 YOUR SUPPORT' on the back, must have cost a five-figure sum. Their effect was priceless.

— COWAN'S CAPTURE —

Legendary Villa secretary George Ramsay was not averse to using some questionable methods if he was determined to sign a particular player. The circumstances surrounding his recruitment of half-back James Cowan in 1899 are a case in point.

Cowan had originally left his native Vale of Leven club to attend a trial with Warwick County FC, based in the Birmingham suburb of Edgbaston. But Ramsay, upon hearing that a highly regarded fellow-Scot was headed for Birmingham, met Cowan at the railway station, took him to the Old Crown and Cushion Inn which served as his club's headquarters in Perry Barr, and refused to let the player leave until he had agreed to join the Villa.

— OLD FRIENDS —

Aston Villa v Everton (or Everton v Aston Villa) is the most played fixture between top-level clubs in English football. There have been 213 games between the two sides, Villa having won 79, Everton 77 and there have been 57 draws. The aggregate score is Villa 328 Everton 328.

— VILLA'S FIRST LEAGUE SEASON —

Villa's first game in the newly formed Football League was away at Wolves on September 8th 1888. The 1–1 draw saw Villa full-back Gershom Cox credited with the first own goal in league history. Villa finished the season in second place, behind double-winners Preston North End, with 29 points from 22 games. Their average attendance was 4,700 and the season also saw two unwanted distinctions. A crowd of 600 for the game with Accrington is believed to be Villa's second lowest-ever league gate, while an 8–1 defeat away at Blackburn Rovers in the FA Cup remains their heaviest ever in the competition.

— THE FATHER OF THE FOOTBALL LEAGUE —

In the early part of 1888, Villa supporters were not best pleased. With their team the dominant force in Midlands football, most matches tended to be embarrassingly one-sided friendlies that were often called off at short notice because the opposition had been unable to field a team. Villa's attendances were by now often numbering several thousand and supporters would arrive at the club's Wellington Road ground to be met with a poster announcing that the afternoon's game had been postponed.

Disgruntled Villa followers regularly made their feelings known at the Newtown draper's shop of club committee member William McGregor, a dour Scotsman who had moved to Birmingham from Braco, Perthshire, in 1870. McGregor sympathised with their frustrations at having so many Saturday afternoons ruined, and knew that the fledgling game of football needed more than just the fleeting competitiveness of the FA Cup if it were to survive. He took steps to ascertain whether officials of other clubs shared his views. To this end he distributed a letter, the opening lines of which have gone down in football legend:

> *"Every year it is becoming more and more difficult for football clubs of any standing to meet their friendly engagements and even arrange friendly matches. The consequence is that at the last moment, through cup-tie interference, clubs are compelled to take on teams who will not attract the public."*

McGregor invited interested parties to a meeting at Anderton's Hotel, in London's Fleet Street on March 22nd 1888, and the world's first football league was formed. Kicking off on September 8th of that year, the 12 founding members of the Football League were: Accrington, Aston Villa, Blackburn Rovers, Bolton Wanderers, Burnley, Derby County, Everton,

Notts County, Preston North End, Stoke, West Bromwich Albion and Wolverhampton Wanderers.

McGregor went on to chair both the Football League and the FA, and was later President of the League. He died in 1911, by which time Villa had won the league championship six times and the FA Cup on four occasions.

In recent years McGregor's memory has been marked in a more tangible form. The Aston Villa Supporters Trust commissioned a statue of the great man, which stands on the forecourt to the Trinity Road stand, and also arranged for the grave of him and his wife Jessie to be renovated in time for a service to mark the centenary of his death. This took place at St Mary's church, Handsworth, where they are buried, on December 20th 2011 and, like his funeral, was attended by footballing and civic dignitaries from around the country.

— THE BEST VILLA TEAM EVER? —

Villa may have won the league title on seven occasions, and a total of 20 major trophies, but what was arguably the most exciting Villa team of the lot never won a thing.

The 1930/31 team included legendary centre-forward Pongo Waring (See *Great Villains: Pongo Waring*, page 47) who scored 49 during the season, a club record, while Eric Houghton, then known as having the hardest shot in football, scored 30 from the wing. With inside-forward Billy Walker, Villa's record goalscorer and the man reckoned by many to be the club's greatest-ever player, and the half-back line of Gibson, Talbot and Tate the most efficient midfield in football, it was going to take something special to stop the Villa.

Unfortunately, Arsenal's 1930/31 team was not only their equal on the field, the Gunners also possessed in Herbert Chapman the first great football manager. Chapman was every bit as much a visionary as had been the Villa triumvirate of Rinder, Ramsay and McGregor 30 years earlier, and was the main reason why his team condemned their Astonian rivals to the runners-up spot (and did so again two years later).

Villa's great team finished second in the First Division in 1930/31, despite scoring a top flight record 128 goals, 86 of which came from just 21 home games (both league games between the sides ended with the home side scoring five). Indeed, Sheffield United, who finished third, scored 102 and the overall number of goals scored in that season's top tier was 1,823, which worked out at an average of almost four a game. Of the 462 First Division games played in 1930/31, just 13 were goalless draws.

— INTERNATIONAL DUTY —

Villa have had 74 players capped by England, more than any other club. The first were Arthur Brown and Howard Vaughton, who both played against Ireland on February 18th 1882. England won 13–0, with Vaughton scoring five goals and Brown four.

The full list of Villa's England internationals is as follows:

Gabriel Agbonlahor (3 appearances), Albert Allen (1), Charlie Athersmith (12), Joe Bache (7), Earl Barrett (2), Frank Barson (1), Gareth Barry (29), Darren Bent (3), Joe Beresford (1), George Blackburn (1), Billy Brawn (2), Frank Broome (8), Arthur Brown (3), George Brown (1), Scott Carson (2), Stan Collymore (1), Gordon Cowans (8), James Crabtree (11), Tony Daley (7), John Devey (2), Arthur Dorrell (4), Stewart Downing (4), Dion Dublin (1), Andy Ducat (3), Ugo Ehiogu (1), Tommy Gardner (2), Billy Garraty (1), Billy George (1), Colin Gibson (1), John Gidman (1), Albert Hall (1), Harry Hampton (2), Sam Hardy (9), Lee Hendrie (1), Emile Heskey (12), Gerry Hitchens (3), Steve Hodge (11), Denny Hodgetts (6), Eric Houghton (7), David James (4), Billy Kirton (1), Alex Leake (5), Brian Little (1), Eddie Lowe (3), Jack Martin (2), Paul Merson (1), James Milner (12), Tony Morley (6), Tommy Mort (3), Frank Moss (5), Ben Olney (4), David Platt (22), John Reynolds (7), Kevin Richardson (1), Tommy Smart (5), Leslie Smith (2), Steve Smith (1), Gareth Southgate (42), Howard Spencer (6), Nigel Spink (1), Ronnie Starling (1), Joe Tate (3), Tommy Thompson (1), Darius Vassell (22), Howard Vaughton (4), Billy Walker (18), Charlie Wallace (3), Thomas Waring (5), Ollie Whatley (2), Fred Wheldon (4), Albert Wilkes (3), Peter Withe (11), Dickie Yorke (2), Ashley Young (15).

— GREAT VILLANS: GEORGE RAMSAY —

The greatest Villa man of all?

There are many who could argue that they were the greatest Villa man of all, but one who has perhaps the strongest claim to the title is George Burrell Ramsay. Born in the Scottish village of Ayon't' the Tweed, in 1855, Ramsay came to Birmingham at the age of 21, and while out walking one afternoon in 1876, came across a group of young men who were playing football on Aston Park. Legend has it that several games of football were taking place in the park that day, but only one team was a man short. Had any of the other sides been short of numbers, football history may have been very different. Ramsay begged a game with a team who informed him they were called Aston Villa, and soon drew their admiration with a display of ball control that far exceeded the kick-and-rush tactics employed by the fledgling team who were soon begging him to join their number.

Ramsay agreed to join the Villa club, teaching his new teammates the skills he had learned as a boy, and under his captaincy they won their first trophy, the Birmingham Senior Cup of 1880.

Injury forced Ramsay to retire from playing the game at the age of 25, but he remained a committee member and then secretary, soon showing himself to be perhaps the greatest administrator in the history of the game. It was Ramsay who saw the need for Villa to have a ground of their own, securing a lease on the Wellington Road enclosure at Perry Barr where Villa first made their name. Ramsay possessed the finest eye for raw talent of his time, and could lure both unknown and highly-regarded players to Villa by a mixture of charm, flattery and occasionally kidnap (see *Cowan's Capture*, page 7). In conjunction with his equally visionary committee colleagues William McGregor and Frederick Rinder, Ramsay set about making Aston Villa the biggest name in football.

At the time of Ramsay's retirement in 1926, he had been club secretary for 42 years. Given that such a role then involved much of what would be considered managerial responsibilities these days, Ramsay could be said to also be the greatest manager English football has ever seen. He died nine years later and is buried in St Mary's churchyard, Handsworth Wood, close to the last resting place of his great friend and colleague, William McGregor.

Ramsay's gravestone reads 'Founder of Aston Villa,' and while this may not be strictly true, it was he, more than anyone else, who made the club pre-eminent masters of the Victorian era.

— YOU DON'T KNOW WHAT YOU'RE DOING —

Villa signed wing-half Jimmy Gibson from Partick Thistle in April 1927, then in the following month bought inside-forward Joe Beresford from Mansfield Town. Both men were astute purchases who gave many years of service to the club. Maybe it was just as well, because neither player knew whom they were joining when they signed for the Villa.

Gibson was heavily influenced by his father, and Partick were so desperate to receive the agreed fee that they informed Gibson senior, who forgot to tell his son that he was bound for the Midlands. Not until meeting Villa chairman Jack Jones and secretary Billy Smith in Glasgow prior to signing did Jimmy think to ask which club he would be joining.

Strange though this tale might have been, Joe Beresford went one better than his new colleague when he joined the club in May of the same year. The boards of Villa and his then-club Mansfield arranged the deal, Joe was called into the boardroom at Mansfield's Field Mill ground and told that he was being transferred. Only after the formalities had been completed did Beresford think to ask the name of his new club. However, as he stayed with the Villa until 1936, he must have been satisfied with his 'decision'.

— CELEBRITY SUPPORTERS —

Mercifully, Villa have avoided the attentions of those embarrassing famous fans who have claimed allegiance to what they invariably call the beautiful game ever since football became fashionable. Violinist Nigel Kennedy came close, but most Villa supporters who knew the score had nothing but respect for him after witnessing the world's greatest living violinist standing on the old open away ends at Chelsea or Crystal Palace, without a retinue of minders, long before Sky Sports came along.

The club has its fair share of well-known fans, many of whom are a cut above the norm, even if some are more dedicated than others. Prince William was spotted at Wembley for Villa's FA Cup semi-final against Bolton in 2000. It's not known what turned the heir to the heir to the throne into a Villa supporter, although suspicion has fallen on an employee at his family home in Gloucestershire. Conservative leader David Cameron has a nominal allegiance to the Villa, thanks to his uncle, former club chairman Sir William Dugdale, and attended a Premier League game at Queens Park Rangers during 2011/12. Governor of the Bank of England, Mervyn King, is a Villa Park regular and a patron of the Aston Villa Supporters Trust.

Other famous Villa supporters include poet Benjamin Zephaniah, Black Sabbath bass player Geezer Butler, local historian and broadcaster Professor Carl Chinn, football grounds expert Simon Inglis and former Home Secretary Jacqui Smith. The unlikeliest of all Villa's celebrity supporters, though, must be Hollywood actor Tom Hanks, who once said that his reason for following the Villa was that "the name is so sweet . . . like a lovely spa." Tom has never been spotted on the Holte End.

— AGAINST THE ODDS —

Villa were drawn at home at Wimbledon in the fourth round of the FA Cup in 1992/93, going out on penalties at Selhurst Park in a replay. Their next home draw was in the fourth round against West Bromwich Albion, five seasons later. In the meantime, Villa were drawn away in twelve successive ties. The odds against this happening are 4,095 to 1.

— GOING HOME —

When Villa were first formed they played home games at Wilson Road, and then at the Aston Lower Grounds. There was nothing regular in these arrangements; the club would find the most convenient area of grassland in what was then a semi-rural area much removed from the grime of industrial Birmingham, and mark out a football pitch.

Their first permanent home was Wellington Road, Perry Barr, to where the club moved in 1876. The field on which the ground stood was hired for £5 per annum from a local butcher, and the team changed in a nearby blacksmith's forge. The pitch had a haystack in the middle, which the team had to clear before each game, a hump near one goal and a line of trees along a touchline. Yet despite these deficiencies, the ground was considered fit to host games in both the FA Cup and in the early days of the Football League.

Wellington Road also played host to several important fixtures, such as an amateur international versus Ireland in 1893, as well as witnessing one of the first instances of crowd problems, when the cavalry had to be called from the nearby Great Brook Street barracks to help maintain order at an FA Cup fifth round tie versus Preston in 1888. Overcrowding rather than disorder had been the cause of the problem, with a record 27,000 in attendance, but nevertheless the match was abandoned after a succession of pitch invasions with Preston 3–1 ahead. The FA subsequently ordered that the result should stand.

Villa's success led to their landlord demanding ever-increasing sums, and when he put their rent up to £200, the committee decided that the time was right to find a new home. In 1897 they moved to the Aston Lower Grounds, opposite their old makeshift headquarters in Aston Park. There is no remaining trace of the old ground at Perry Barr, although the wall of a local garage contains the outline of an archway that, as legend has it, was the entrance to the blacksmith's premises where the teams would get changed.

The new ground, later to become known as Villa Park, was leased from brewers Flowers & Co at £250 per annum, for a period of 21 years, although the club were able to purchase the ground outright for the sum of five shillings per square yard in 1911.

The only other ground on which Villa have hosted a competitive first-team fixture is, ironically, the Hawthorns, where they played Intertoto games against Dukla Pribram and Celta Vigo in July 2000, as Villa Park was unavailable due to the building of the new Trinity Road stand. They have also played an away game at Villa Park, when the FA Cup third round tie with Southern League Gravesend and Northfleet was switched in January 1996.

— KITTED OUT —

The rampant lion

The origins of Villa's traditional claret and blue colours will probably never be categorically explained, although there are several theories, some more credible than others (See *The Great Mysteries*, page 100). It is, though, agreed that the strong Caledonian influence of such men as William McGregor and George Ramsay led to the decision to adopt the Scottish symbol the Lion Rampant as the club's badge soon after the club's formation – Villa being the first football club in England to use this emblem. The lion was at first incorporated into the team's kit design, but due to various difficulties (one contemporary report bemoaning the fact that "our lion had no chance with the washing lady") this idea was scrapped and the Villa shirt lacked a club badge until well into the 1950s.

The club occasionally experimented with different designs in those early years, most notably chocolate and light blue, but settled on the familiar claret body and blue arms during the mid-1890s. This basic design remained unaltered for around 90 years, until the later part of the 1980s, when Villa began experimenting with a series of kit variations. Some, such as the 1989/90 design or retro 1992/93 effort, were traditional. Others, most notably the half-and-half fiasco of the late eighties and the assortment of stripes the club occasionally foisted on supporters as commercial interest began to hold sway, were clearly not. Fortunately, recent kit designs have seen a move back to the basic design associated with a Villa shirt. Long may this fashion last.

— GREAT VILLANS: DENNIS MORTIMER —

Dennis Mortimer and friend

Dennis Mortimer was born on Merseyside on April 5th 1952, attending the same school as another future European Cup winner, Phil Thompson of Liverpool, and appearing for the Kirkby Boys team alongside his future team-mate Kenny Swain. He signed for Coventry City and joined Villa shortly before Christmas 1975 for what was then a club record fee of £175,000. Mortimer was the first of the European Cup side to make his debut for the Villa and named team captain in succession to Leighton Phillips, in 1979.

The driving force of Villa's midfield, Mortimer was chiefly remembered for his surging runs, one of which led to the second goal of Villa's 2–0 win at home to Liverpool in January 1981, generally regarded as the defining moment of that season's title win. Together with Gordon Cowans and Des Bremner he led the powerhouse midfield trio that inspired Villa's early eighties success. The pictures of Dennis Mortimer holding up the European Cup in de Kuip stadium, Rotterdam, remain the most vivid images of the greatest night in Villa history.

Mortimer once said of the team he led to glory, "The hardest part of captaining that team was tossing the coin and picking up the trophies," but he offered much more. Tony Morley says, "Dennis *was* Aston Villa at that time. Ron Saunders told him what to do and Dennis did it. You looked for Dennis for inspiration and you knew what you were getting."

Mortimer was probably the most extreme example of the scandalous way in which Villa's team of the early eighties were ignored by their international managers. Despite captaining the England B team, the closest he ever got to full honours was a place on the bench for the 1981 Home Internationals with Scotland and Wales and he is widely regarded as the finest uncapped English player of the modern era.

Mortimer emulated Charlie Aitken's feat of winning the Villa Player of the Year award twice, in 1976/77 and again in 1983/84. However, he fell victim to new manager Graham Turner's desire to rebuild the following season and, after a spell on loan to Sheffield United, a free transfer to Brighton ended the Villa career of the club's most successful captain since John Devey at the turn of the century. His final game in a Villa shirt came in the Birmingham Senior Cup final, when Villa reserves defeated non-league Wednesfield Social. Not only was this Villa's first victory in the competition since 1912, but a sporting gesture by captain Dean Glover allowed Mortimer the chance to lift the final trophy of a glittering career. He had played 405 first-team games, scoring 36 goals.

After a year at Brighton, Mortimer went on to spend a season playing alongside his former Villa midfield colleague Des Bremner at Birmingham City. He joined Albion as community officer, rising to the post of assistant manager, managed the Wolves ladies team for a while and is now employed by the PFA.

A controversial character because of his outspoken views on Villa matters, Mortimer was a fierce critic of former chairman Doug Ellis although he has regularly offered his full support to owner at the time of writing Randy Lerner.

— DEADLY'S VARIED CAREER —

Doug Ellis didn't spend his entire working life solely as Villa chairman. He has also, according to Doug, been a market trader, trainee journalist, shorthand teacher, head chorister of Chester Cathedral, schoolboy boxing champion of the Wirral, Cheshire under-18s table-tennis player, farmer, professional footballer with Crewe Alexandra, Tranmere Rovers and Southport, commander of a transport division during World War II, railway ticket collector, promoter of Birmingham Speedway, chairman of Wolverhampton Wanderers, director of Birmingham City, chairman of the Good Hope Hospital Trust, travel agent, inventor of the bicycle kick, the man who popularised package holidays, author, builder, brewer, property developer, Knight Bachelor and Member of the Most Excellent Order of the British Empire.

Some of these are undoubtedly true, others are dubious (for example, the Professional Footballers Association has no record of a Herbert Douglas Ellis ever having played professionally) and some cannot be proved one way or the other.

— VILLA'S FIRST SUBSTITUTE —

The record books state that the first Villa player to come on as a substitute was Graham Parker during a 3–2 at home to Spurs on 25th September 1965. However, there was one earlier Villa player who took part in a game he didn't start. On 26th November 1898 Villa travelled to Sheffield to play Wednesday in a league fixture. With just over ten minutes to go, the game was abandoned due to the light being too bad for play to continue. Wednesday were winning 3–1 and in those days there was no provision for replaying such matches; the result at the time of the abandonment was generally accepted as standing. However, with Villa in the running for the league title they refused to accept this decision – whereupon the Football League announced that the remaining 10½ minutes would be played at a later date and that any player eligible for the first game could play in the second. Wednesday made six changes but Villa made just one – Billy Garraty replacing Frank Bedingfield, who was ironically their goalscorer in the first part of the match. In the remainder of play Wednesday scored once more to officially be recorded as 4–1 winners, but Villa had the last laugh as they went on to win that season's First Division title while the home side were subsequently relegated. This was Bedingfield's only game for the Villa and he moved to Queens Park Rangers at the end of the season, while Garraty went on to become one of the great Villa forwards, a mainstay of the side which also won the following year's league championship and the 1905 FA Cup.

— RANDY LERNER: A HISTORY —

Randy Lerner was born in Brooklyn, New York, in 1962. The son of Alfred Lerner, owner of the MBNA credit card business, and his wife Norma, Lerner graduated from Columbia University in 1984, after having spent time at Cambridge a year earlier. It was while studying in Britain that he reputedly developed an interest in English football. Prior to entering the business world he worked as a lawyer in New York then joined insurance company Progressive Corporation as an investment analyst.

In 1991 Lerner started up an investment company, Securities Advisers Inc, becoming a director of MBNA two years later. His father's death in 2001 saw Lerner become chairman of MBNA, a position he retained after their merger with the Bank of America.

Prior to taking over the Villa, Lerner was best known in sporting circles for his ownership of the Cleveland Browns franchise in the National Football League of the USA. Lerner's father was regarded as a hero in Cleveland after he returned the team to their home town following a period from 1996–99 when the team was deactivated and the players moved to a new Baltimore franchise. Randy has continued to take a keen interest in the Browns and despite their regular lack of success, his fan-friendly attitude has enabled Lerner to retain his popularity amongst Browns supporters.

Lerner bought a controlling interest in Aston Villa in October 2006, and soon gained 100% control. As with the Browns, his attitude towards supporters and respect for the club and its traditions have made him a hugely popular figure amongst Villa supporters. Soon after taking control of the club, for example, he showed his generosity by providing around 5,000 fans with free coach travel to Villa's Carling Cup tie at Chelsea.

Lerner has three children and has a reputed net worth of $1.6 billion, although the Lerner family trust is allegedly worth many times this figure.

— AKA —

Some Villa players down the years have been better known by their nicknames:

Len **'King'** Capewell
Thomas **'Pongo'** Waring
Ian **'Chico'** Hamilton
Gordon **'Sid'** Cowans
'Happy' Harry Hampton
Ernest **'Mush'** Callaghan
Ken **'K.O.'** Roberts
Stan **'the Wham'** Lynn

— THEY SAID IT —

"For brilliance and for consistency of achievement, for astute management and for general alertness, the superiors of Aston Villa cannot be found."

William McGregor, Aston Villa committee member and founder of the Football League

"Since we have been attending football matches we have never been witness to such disgraceful scenes."

The *Birmingham Evening Mail* reporting on the cup-tie with Preston which ended in the cavalry being called upon to restore order, 1888

"We are not talking about a mere business. This is the Aston Villa Football Club and it deserves nothing but the best."

Frederick Rinder, club chairman, 1924

"The famous Villa club is the outstanding professional football organisation of the world."

Football Encyclopaedia, 1934

"Aston Villa will play in the European Cup one day."

Tommy Docherty, after being sacked as team manager, 1970

"Why didn't you just belt it?"

Barbara Southgate after her son, Villa's Gareth, missed THAT penalty for England v Germany in Euro 96

"There's an aura about this club, a sense of history and tradition. Even the name is beautifully symmetrical, with five letters in each word."

John Gregory, as Villa manager

"Aston Villa always seem to have problems taking the final step toward being a really big club."

Graham Taylor, shortly before returning as a director in 2001

"I think they're great."

HRH Prince William on Villa

"WE'RE NOT FICKLE – WE JUST DON'T LIKE YOU."

Banner in the Holte End after David O'Leary had called Villa supporters 'fickle'

— VILLA AGAINST THE NAZIS —

During the summer of 1938, Villa were invited to take part in a tour of Germany. This was not surprising – they were the most famous club in the world and manager Jimmy Hogan had enjoyed great success throughout Europe as a coach prior to arriving at Villa Park.

Adolph Hitler's ambitions were beginning to give cause for concern through Europe, but the full horrors of the Nazi regime had yet to be discovered, so there was little comment when Villa agreed to the tour, which would comprise of three matches against selected German opposition. On May 14th 1938, an England team including Villa centre-forward Frank Broome played against Germany in the Olympic Stadium, Berlin, winning 6–3. Before the game the England team, acting on advice from the Foreign Office, performed a Nazi salute to a packed house of 110,000, who roared their approval.

On the following day, Villa played in the same stadium against an even stronger German Select XI, which included players from the recently annexed Austria, and were also advised to make the Nazi salute. The players refused and this supposed lack of manners was heavily criticised in the German press. Villa won the game 3–2. The following game was in Stuttgart, also against a German Select XI, and following representations from the German government, Foreign Office diplomats were more insistent in their demands that the Villa players paid tribute to their hosts before their 1–0 victory.

Inside-forward Eric Houghton recalled, in Rogan Taylor's book *Kicking and Screaming*, that, "Both teams did the Nazi salute, then we went to the centre of the field and gave the two-fingered salute. And they cheered like mad . . . they didn't know what it meant."

The inference was clear; Villa players had been asked to give a Nazi salute voluntarily, and refused. They were then ordered to do so, and performed a salute – after a fashion. Their later gestures made it quite clear that they had little but contempt for the politics of their hosts.

This was the accepted story for many years, until in 2001 the *Sunday Mercury*, for some reason, chose to make a front page story of the fact that a photograph had been unearthed which showed Villa players apparently making a Nazi salute in Stuttgart. The newspaper stated that the club had denied the story for years and instead had claimed their players had refused to salute altogether. The newspaper's inference was that Villa had deliberately lied to cover up the incident, which had never been the case.

Despite this bit of unnecessary muck-raking, Villa supporters continue to regard the actions of their players at that time as in keeping with the finest traditions of the club. They were asked to show support for the Nazi regime, and refused. They were ordered to do so by the British and German governments, and did as little as they could, with reluctance and under enormous pressure. Such behaviour is deserving of the greatest respect.

— GREAT GAMES 1: THE GREATEST MATCH EVER —

Aston Villa 4	**Manchester United 6**
Edwards (2)	Rowley
Dorsett	Morris (2)
Smith	Pearson (2)
	Delaney

January 10th 1948: FA Cup Third Round
Villa Park
Att: 58,683

Villa have taken part in many great footballing occasions. However, the game most regularly described as the greatest ever by those who were in attendance wasn't a cup final, a European glory night or a vital league clash. Villa didn't even win the match.

In January 1948, Villa played Manchester United at home in the third round of the FA Cup. A crowd of more than 58,000 were in attendance and the majority of them were in raptures when, straight from the kick-off, Villa took the ball downfield and George Edwards hit the back of the net with a shot that left United keeper Crompton stranded. The goal was timed at 13 and a half seconds and no United player had touched the ball.

Crompton might have been helpless to stop Edwards' strike, but he had little else to do for the rest of the first half. United's inside-forwards fed their wingers with repeated, perfectly-placed balls which the Villa full-backs Potts and Parkes could do little to curtail. United scored five times, and as the sides left the field the tie looked over.

But the Villa were not regarded as the greatest cup-fighting side in England for no reason. Two quick goals brought with them the scent of a remarkable comeback, as the heavy pitch gave assistance to the home side's superior strength and nullified the visitors' greater passing ability.

Dickie Dorsett hit home a penalty to make the score 5–4 in the 81st minute and the greatest revival of all time seemed likely. Everyone in the crowd was now screaming their enthusiasm, even those few neutrals having been bowled along on a wave of euphoria. When Trevor Ford rose above the United defence to meet a perfectly-placed cross from the wing, it seemed as though the comeback was complete. But the ball crashed against the crossbar, bounced around the penalty area and was hooked clear by a United defender.

The resulting breakaway led to a corner, from which inside-forward Pearson made sure of victory with United's sixth. The final whistle sounded seconds later, and the crowd rose to applaud the weary players back to the dressing rooms.

Veteran *Times* football correspondent Geoffrey Green wrote in his match report that after witnessing such an exhibition, "I would have been quite satisfied to be put in a box and buried ten feet in the ground" and many years later would still regard the afternoon as his greatest footballing memory.

— VILLA PARK I: TRINITY ROAD —

"Would anyone argue against the assertion that the Trinity Road entrance of Villa Park has more pomp and style than that of any other ground?" These were the words of Villa fan Simon Inglis in his book *The Football Grounds of England and Wales*, back in 1985.

Designed by Archibald Leitch, the greatest football architect of all time, the Trinity Road stand represented an era when Aston Villa were the foremost club in the world. No expense had been spared in its construction, with stained glass windows, mosaics, central roof gable and curved wooden balcony. There was also an oak-panelled dining room, while the pavilion towers and central stairway emulated Aston Hall and the great public buildings of the city.

Opened in 1924 to replace the original tin-roofed terrace which had stood since Villa Park had been built 27 years earlier, the stand held 6,500 in tip-up seats upstairs with terrace space for another 11,000 in the downstairs enclosure. Yet costs had escalated from their original estimates and when the bill was eventually revealed to stand at almost £65,000, chairman Fredrick Rinder was forced to resign his post. Rinder had built a monument, but had paid for it with his removal from office.

The Trinity Road stand stood for over 75 years. While the roof was patched up and seats replaced when necessary, it remained almost unchanged until 1971, when 3,800 seats were installed into the downstairs enclosure at a cost of £21,000, together with 17 executive boxes. So popular were these boxes that the £36,000 cost of their building was covered by the first three-year lease period.

Safety legislation meant that modernisation of the stand would be necessary towards the end of the twentieth century. In the summer of 1992 two bays were added to the outside towers, with the central stairway rebuilt and new corporate areas opened. On the upper tier the old wooden floors were recovered and plastic seats replaced the original wooden ones. The cost of this redevelopment was £2.4 million, and it was thought that the stand would be fit to give many more years service.

However, within eight years the entire structure had gone. The board decided that the ground needed refurbishing and the old, much-loved Trinity Road stand was declared to be standing in the way of progress. Despite a belief that the stand was in some way a listed building, no such protection was in place and to many supporters' anger the entire structure – mosaics, gable, stained glass and all – was demolished in the summer of 2000.

In its place came a three-tier development officially opened by Prince Charles in November 2001. Built at a cost of £17 million, the stand has room for 13,000 supporters, all of whom enjoy a perfect view of the pitch, unlike the cramped and obstructed views of the old stand. It also has a unique feature in English football in that it is built over Trinity Road and extends into Aston Park. But modern as it is, the new stand will never have the character of its predecessor.

— ON THE DAY WAR BROKE OUT . . . —

Britain officially declared war on September 3rd 1939. The Football League programme was immediately cancelled and on 26th September the Villa players decided to disband the club for the duration of the war – the first club to do so. In contrast, Birmingham FC (as they were then still known) were the only club whose players wished to continue but their efforts were thwarted when the Chief Constable of Birmingham banned them from using St Andrews.

Villa regrouped for a testimonial in aid of Blues goalkeeper Harry Hibbs when the two sides met at St Andrews in April 1940 (the Chief Constable had briefly relented) and formally returned to competitive action of a sort when a Birmingham League was established for the 1940/41 season. All their games were away fixtures, and with most footballers either in the army or in similar occupations guest players were commonplace; amateur clubs with nearby barracks or aerodromes often found themselves fielding a team of established professionals. Villa finished seventh in the nine-team league, losing to such opposition as Wellington Town, Revo Athletic and Worcester City, the latter on five occasions.

Villa Park reopened in September 1941 and the team's fortunes subsequently improved, winning the league and the Birmingham Cup amongst other semi-official competitions. As the threat of air raids receded, crowds grew and the Football League War Cup became a regular fixture in the calendar. In 1944 Villa beat Blackpool over two legs to win the northern section and drew 1–1 with Charlton in the final, played at Stamford Bridge, to share the trophy.

— INTERNATIONAL DUTY —

Villa Park is the only ground to have staged England internationals in three different centuries. It hosted England's 2–1 victory over Scotland in 1899, seven England internationals in the twentieth century, and friendlies with Spain in 2001, Portugal the following year and the Netherlands in 2005. Villa Park was also the venue for games in the 1966 World Cup, Euro 96 (including the Czech Republic v Portugal quarter-final) and Sweden v Brazil in 1995.

— CARLOS KICKABALL —

It's not unusual these days for foreign players to make their way into the English game by persuading gullible clubs that they're a star back in their homeland. But as with many things, Villa were caught out in this way years before other clubs.

Argentinian midfielder Oscar Arce joined the Villa in 1968. The *Villa News and Record* stated that Arce was so determined to play for the club that he completed a two-year residential qualification in this country before he came along and asked to be taken on the payroll. He didn't bother to find out first whether he would make the grade, he just spent two years in Britain then popped along to Villa Park to sign on. For that reason alone the club ought to have been wary. His real name was Luis, but maybe he chose Oscar because he was the greatest actor to appear in claret and blue.

Arce claimed to be an Argentinian international, and Villa were so impressed with his CV that nobody checked which Argentine team he had played for, or if indeed he played for any national team at all, not least a football one. He claimed to have played for Uruguayan giants Penarol, and that was enough for Villa to be seduced.

Arce sat out the first few games of 1968/69 before making his first appearance on the hallowed turf in a reserve match against Stoke City at inside left. Those who saw the game reported that he was useless. The team sheet for his fourth reserve game also included a certain H. Arce, Oscar's brother Hector. After a couple of games Hector came to be recorded as H Fullone (Arce) before the bracketed name was dropped.

Oscar was substituted at half-time on his brother's debut but then played in three more games before the penny finally dropped that Villa had been taken for a ride. Hector played a dozen games for the reserves, but despite a comparatively longer career than his brother, faded from the collective memory of Villa supporters.

Oscar was released in January 1969 and, with Aston Villa now on his CV, moved to Scotland, where he seemed to play for a different team every week before disappearing into obscurity.

— EE AYE ADDIO WE LOST THE CUP —

'We was robbed!'

In April 1895 Villa beat West Bromwich Albion 1–0 in the FA Cup final at Crystal Palace, to win the trophy for the second time.

In the early part of September that year, the club allowed local football boot manufacturer William Shillcock to display the trophy in the window of his shop in Newtown Row. And that was the last they saw of the original FA Cup. Some time between Shillcock locking up at 9.30pm on Wednesday September 11th and returning to the premises at 7.30am the following day, thieves broke into the shop and made off with the trophy, together with a sum of cash.

Notices were posted around the city appealing for information leading to the cup's return or the arrest of the miscreants and a £10 reward offered. But honour must have been prevalent amongst late-Victorian Brummie thieves and the crime was never solved. Villa had insured the cup for £200, the amount they had guaranteed the FA as a safe-keeping bond and were ordered to buy a new trophy, which was made by Messrs Vaughtons of Hockley (and eventually itself replaced in 1911), as well as being fined £25.

And there, for many years, the story ended, until one morning in February 1958, when the *Sunday Pictorial* carried on its front page a 'confession' from Harry Burge, an 83-year-old inmate of a Birmingham City Corporation nursing home.

Burge claimed that it had been he who, all those years ago, had broken into Shillcock's shop and, along with two accomplices, taken the cup, together with several pairs of boots and cash from the till. They had then gone to Burge's nearby house and melted down the cup to make counterfeit half-crowns, some of which had been passed in the Salutation public house, then owned by Villa winger Dennis Hodgetts. Birmingham City police made enquiries and stated that the old man's memory was none too reliable, although they did disclose that he had spent 46 years in jail since first being convicted of theft in 1897. Burge said his reason for the confession was that he was an old man and the theft had been on his conscience for too long. Presumably, the fee paid to him by the *Pictorial* had also helped loosen his tongue.

And there ended one of the strangest stories in football history. There was, though, a reminder when Villa won the European Cup in 1982 and the trophy was taken to a supporters club function in Derbyshire, only to go missing and be found, the following morning, on the steps of a police station in Sheffield. Villa, as fans like to remind their less-fortunate neighbours, have lost more trophies than the Blues have won.

— THE AWOL HALF-BACK —

Once James Cowan had been 'forced' into signing for the Villa (see *Cowan's Capture*, page 7), he settled down into the first team and became by common consent the finest centre-half of his day. Not only was Cowan fierce in the tackle and an excellent header of the ball, he was one of the quickest footballers the club has ever fielded. So fast could Cowan run that, during the early part of the 1895/96 season, he began to entertain thoughts of winning a lucrative sprint race held in Edinburgh, the Powderhall Sprint Handicap.

The big problem with this idea was that the race took place in January, during the height of the football season, and Cowan knew that his club would never allow him time off to return to Scotland in order to undergo the necessary training. He therefore complained of a back injury, and insisted on being sent to his native Jamestown, in the Vale of Leven, to recover.

The club reluctantly agreed to Cowan's request and let him return home with orders to be examined by a local doctor. The doctor insisted that he could find nothing wrong with Cowan's back, but equally felt unable to accuse such a famous footballer of malingering, and so informed the Villa that the player was, indeed, injured.

Had the doctor not been short-sighted he would have soon found all the evidence he needed to substantiate his initial suspicions, for Cowan, unfamiliar with the area after several years away, later admitted that he ran past the medical man's house one evening while on a training run. Luckily for him, the doctor failed to recognise the player and was therefore unable to congratulate himself on the quickest recovery from injury ever known to medical science.

By the time of the race, word had reached Birmingham of Cowan's subterfuge, and several of his team-mates, including Charlie Athersmith, Bob Chatt and Albert Evans, had travelled to Edinburgh to support their colleague. As an 'unknown' sprinter, Cowan received the maximum start of 12 ½ yards in the 130 yard race, and won the first prize of £80 with ease. His Villa colleagues were less fortunate. They should have made more than enough money betting on the race to pay for their excursion, but unfortunately James Cowan proved to be only the second-quickest man in Edinburgh that day as the bookmaker with whom the Villa players had laid their bets welched and left them penniless.

Cowan returned to Birmingham to face the wrath of a Villa committee furious at the way in which they had been tricked. He was promptly suspended for four weeks. But even Villa's autocratic patriarchs had to appreciate his ingenuity and the suspension was soon lifted, enabling Cowan to take his place in the double-winning side of the following season.

— CHAMPIONS II: 1895/96 —

Villa's second league title in was built around their invincible home form, with a record of 14 wins and a single draw from 15 games. This was the only season in which they remained unbeaten in league fixtures at Perry Barr.

	P	W	D	L	F	A	Pts
Aston Villa	**30**	**20**	**5**	**5**	**78**	**45**	**45**
Derby County	30	17	7	6	68	35	41
Everton	30	16	7	7	66	43	39
Bolton Wanderers	30	16	5	9	49	37	37
Sunderland	30	15	7	8	52	41	37
Stoke	30	15	0	15	56	47	30
Sheffield Wednesday	30	12	5	13	44	53	29
Blackburn Rovers	30	12	5	13	40	50	29
Preston North End	30	11	6	13	44	48	28
Burnley	30	10	7	13	48	44	27
Bury	30	12	3	15	50	54	27
Sheffield United	30	10	6	14	40	50	26
Nottingham Forest	30	11	3	16	42	57	25
Wolverhampton Wanderers	30	10	1	19	61	65	21
Small Heath	30	8	4	18	39	79	20
West Bromwich Albion	30	6	7	17	30	59	19

— GOAL OF THE SEASON —

Villa players have won the *Match of the Day* 'Goal of the Season' competition on two occasions. The first was Tony Morley's long range effort away at Everton on February 2nd 1981. This was followed 12 seasons later by Dalian Atkinson's superb solo goal at Wimbledon on October 3rd 1992.

— GREAT VILLANS: RON SAUNDERS —

The greatest

After a playing career during which he became one of Portsmouth's greatest-ever forwards (157 goals in 258 games), Ron Saunders turned his hand to management. He started out with non-league Yeovil Town and then Oxford United of the Second Division, before moving to the highest level, first with Norwich City and then Manchester City. He achieved the notable feat of taking the latter two clubs to consecutive League Cup finals, losing with Norwich in 1973 and City the following year. A fall-out with the playing staff at Manchester City led to Saunders' dismissal and subsequent appointment as Villa manager in June 1974.

His effect on the club was instant. Promotion back to the First Division was achieved in his first season while Saunders' third League Cup final in a row saw him a winner at last, as his former side Norwich were beaten 1–0 at Wembley.

Two years later, what many regard as Villa's best post-war

team won the League Cup again, beating Everton 3–2 in a second replay at Old Trafford and finishing fourth in the league, Villa's highest placing for over forty years.

Saunders then spent three seasons battling with player discontent, appalling luck with injuries and boardroom upheavals before unveiling the culmination of his life's work. The likes of Andy Gray and John Gidman were sold for big money and replaced with youngsters from Villa's 1980 FA Youth Cup winning team and unheralded signings brought in at a fraction of the cost of those whose positions they took.

The Villa side of 1980/81 was unfairly maligned, but neither they nor their manager seemed particularly bothered by criticism as they won the league title by four points, holding their nerve while nearest rivals Ipswich Town crumbled. Their manager's achievement was made even more praiseworthy when considering that the entire 14-man squad that won the title cost little more than the £1.5 million received from Wolves for Andy Gray the previous season.

Saunders' sides were regularly criticised for lack of flair, but the likes of Brian Little, Gary Shaw and Tony Morley were allowed to flourish under his management while the 1976/77 side which scored over a hundred goals was the most attractive in the league.

1981/82 saw league performances dip, but the team marched on throughout Europe. Then on the evening of February 9th 1982 came the sensational news that Saunders had resigned as Villa manager. The reasons were unclear, but while supporters initially reacted with fury, they were astounded when Saunders was appointed Birmingham City manager within a fortnight.

His time at St Andrews was a controversial one, with the Blues relegated, promoted and then doomed to relegation once more when he left the club in January 1986. Saunders became Albion manager but was unable to prevent them going down to the Second Division with the Blues nor to take them back up again the following season. He left the Hawthorns in September 1987 and has scarcely been seen or heard of since.

The way in which Villa under Doug Ellis ignored the achievements of their greatest manager was disgraceful, but Saunders seemed to prefer anonymity. He finally made a re-appearance before a game in December 2006, receiving a tumultuous ovation from a Villa Park crowd who were finally able to give one of the greatest names in the club's history the acclamation he deserved.

Saunders later broke his media silence, telling the *Birmingham Mail* that he resigned because he felt the board lacked respect for him and trust in his abilities. But one suspects that this was nowhere near the full story.

— ASTON ALLITERATIVES —

A team comprised of former Villa players with the same first and second initials:

Kevin Keelan

John Johnstone   Colin Calderwood   Steve Staunton   Albert Aldridge

Billy Baxter   George Graham   Fabio Ferraresi   William (Billy) Walker

Harry Hampton   Tommy Thompson

— RICHES TO RAGS —

Villa won the FA Cup for the first time in 1887, beating West Bromwich Albion in the final. It's fair to say that none of the next Villa team to win the trophy will ever have to work again, but things were different back then. None of that side of 1887 earned much from the game, and one of them, Joey Simmonds, fared worse than the rest. In June 1888, barely 12 months after winning what was then the most prestigious trophy in football, Simmonds was declared bankrupt after the failure of the shop he had bought three years earlier. His assets were given as £79 and his liabilities £154. Modern footballers would spend such amounts without batting an eyelid.

— BOARDROOM BATTLES: PART ONE —

By 1892, Villa's claim to be one of the finest teams in the country was looking shaky. They had struggled at the wrong end of the league table for two seasons, been knocked out of the FA Cup in the early stages, and were in financial difficulties that, rumour had it, were caused in part by gatemen pocketing admission fees at their Wellington Road ground. Frederick Rinder, a member of the Aston Villa committee since 1881, was far from satisfied with the situation and gathered enough support from club members to call an Extraordinary General Meeting that was held at Barwick Street, in the city centre.

Here he lambasted the old men who had overseen the Villa's decline since their FA Cup triumph of 1887, with the result that the committee resigned en bloc. Their replacements included Rinder as financial secretary, and his first decision in this capacity was to install turnstiles at the ground. Matchday takings shot up from £75 to over £200, the club's finances improved, and the next decade saw five League Championships won and the FA Cup twice arriving at Villa Park.

As director and then chairman, Rinder was an integral part of Villa's success before the First World War. But peacetime saw a new generation of shareholders and, lacking Rinder's vision, they began to query his heavy spending. An attempt to oust Rinder from the board in 1921 failed, but three years later his opponents were to have more success, using the excuse of overspending on the Trinity Road stand to force his resignation.

Such was their inability to emulate the great man that 12 years later the club suffered relegation to the Second Division. The Shareholders' Association called another Extraordinary General Meeting, at which they unsuccessfully attempted to add two new members to the board, but the AGM a week later saw the removal of chairman Jack Jones. Rinder returned at the age of 79 and threw himself into the task of reviving the Vila's fortunes, but died two years later, on Christmas Day 1938.

The Villa board then settled into an era of complacency. They ran the club in many ways as it had been run during the Victorian era, secure in the knowledge that these ways had been sufficient to keep Aston Villa at the top. Unfortunately, they were unable to appreciate that football had changed during the intervening decades. The local press regularly poured scorn on the running of the club, but militant supporters, even those who held shares in the Villa, were unable to muster sufficient numbers to cause even the mildest concern in the boardroom.

— CAREER OPPORTUNITIES —

Footballers used to run pubs or newsagents once they retired from the game. Now they work in the media. But there have always been Villa players who went in for more unorthodox careers once they hung up their boots.

Albert Evans: gold prospector in the Yukon
Tony Cascarino: professional gambler
Jim Cumbes: chief executive of Lancashire County Cricket Club
Mike Tindall: preacher
Dr Victor Milne: club doctor
Dick Edwards: country and western singer
Charlie Aitken: antique dealer
Nigel Callaghan: disc jockey
Graham Fenton: fireman

— GREAT GAMES 2: THIRD TIME LUCKY —

Aston Villa 3	**Everton 2**
Little (2)	Lyons
Nicholl	Latchford

13th April 1977 League Cup final 2nd replay
Old Trafford. Att: 54,749

The 1977 League Cup final was one of the most tedious games ever played at Wembley. The first replay at Hillsborough wasn't much better. There had never been a second replay of any English final so no provision had been made for one, which meant it was another four weeks before the game could be played and in that time Villa lost Andy Gray and Frank Carrodus to injury. Everton were now favourites after losing just once in eight games and this status looked justified when a Bob Latchford strike gave them the lead after 38 minutes. As the game moved into the second half it seemed as though Everton would be able to hang onto their lead as the effects of a long season chasing honours on three fronts were beginning to tell on the Villa side. They were, though, keeping their shape and discipline and the supporters who had followed them to north London, Sheffield and now Manchester remained confident even when just ten minutes of the game remained. That's why the team were able to knock the ball around and no one seemed impatient when a six-man move broke down with central defender and captain Chris Nicholl moving out wide to retrieve the ball near the touchline just inside the Everton half. The next few seconds became part of folklore. Nicholl was never exactly known for his close control, but he took the ball past Everton striker Duncan McKenzie, and moved forward to set up another attack. Rather than lay the ball off to a team-mate, Nicholl let fly with a piledriver that was officially reckoned to be from 35 yards out but which gets further with every passing year. Many of those present at the game will now swear that Nicholl was inside his own half when he let fly; some would say the Villa penalty area but that's probably an exaggeration. However far the distance, the ball swerved, dipped and crept inside Everton 'keeper David Lawson's right-hand post. If that wasn't dramatic enough, two minutes later Brian Little collected the ball, beat an Everton defender and from an impossible angle slid the ball past Lawson to give Villa the lead. Still the drama wasn't over when, from the kick-off, Everton took the ball downfield and a defensive mix-up saw Mick Lyons equalise. Both players and supporters were distraught, exhausted, when Alex Cropley picked the ball out of the net, shook his fist and braced everyone for one last effort. All responded in the manner that came to be expected from Ron Saunders' club, but it took until the dying seconds of the game, when a poor ball into the box was missed completely by Everton's Terry Darracott and Brian Little slid home the winner from close range. There was barely time to kick off again and at last the 1977 League Cup final was completed after 330 minutes, spread over 32 days and watched by more than 200,000 spectators. It may have started as the worst final the competition had seen, but it ended as undoubtedly the best.

— GREAT VILLANS: HARRY HAMPTON —

'Appy 'Arry Hampton

Born in April 1885, Hampton was better known as 'Appy 'Arry or the Wellington Whirlwind, after the Shropshire town where he was born.

Hampton joined Villa in 1904 after scoring 54 goals in two seasons for his hometown side Wellington United. He scored twice in Villa's 2–0 win over Newcastle United in the 1905 FA Cup final, and also played in Villa's fifth FA Cup winning final, when they beat Sunderland 1–0 in 1913. Hampton was lucky not to be sent off in this game, as he and Sunderland centre-half Charlie Thomson clashed repeatedly throughout the match, so much so that both men – as well as referee A. Adams – were later suspended for a month by the FA. Hampton also won a league championship medal when Villa took the title in 1909/10, scoring an impressive 29 goals in 35 games.

Hampton was responsible for Villa changing from the dribbling and short passing tactics which had stood them in such good stead to a longer game reliant upon long, sweeping balls out to the wing men and crosses into the penalty area. Here, Hampton would wait to meet either the ball or the opposition goalkeeper with equal relish. Such an aggressive style made him a favourite with the Villa Park crowds, and placed Hampton as Villa's finest centre-forward of their first 50 years.

In total he scored 242 goals in 376 appearances for the Villa, including 14 hat-tricks and five in one game against Sheffield Wednesday in 1912. Only Billy Walker, in over 150 more appearances, has scored more often for the club.

Hampton's top-flight career was interrupted by the outbreak of World War One, which came at a doubly unfortunate time as he had just broken into the England team, winning four caps and scoring twice in 1913 and 1914. He enlisted in the army and survived being gassed at the Somme in 1916.

After the war Hampton joined Birmingham FC, for whom he was top scorer during their Second Division title-winning season of 1920/21, then Newport County before finishing his career back with Wellington United. After retiring he coached Preston North End and Birmingham. He died in March 1963, at the age of 77.

— THE WIT AND WISDOM OF RON ATKINSON —

More words have been said by and about Ron Atkinson than about any other Villa manager. Here's a sample:

"The image is of a big man weighed down with 24 carat jewellery and afloat on a tide of Bollinger."

Evening Mail journalist Leon Hickman

"I played with Ron in about 100 reserve games. And according to Ron he was man of the match in at least 99 of them."

Former Villa player Dennis Jackson, a onetime team-mate of Atkinson's

"I always write Atkinson, D. on the team-sheet. Sometimes I wonder if I'm making a mistake."
On the dilemmas of managers who still play the odd five-a-side

"How can anybody call this work? People in the game don't realise how lucky they are."
Philosophising

"Ron has high ideals. He loves his football and has to like what he sees when his team are playing. If he likes it, he knows the public will too."
Atkinson's former assistant, Dave Sexton

"One of the reserves said to me 'I'm finding it hard – it's the first time I've ever been dropped.' So I said to him 'Do what Nick Faldo does and work at your game.' Next thing I know he's doing exactly what Nick Faldo does. He's taken up golf."
On an unnamed player

"We had a very constructive discussion at half-time. Then I decided to give it the full b******s."
On a typical half-time pep talk

"Kent Nielsen – he was lightning slow."
Describing Villa's Danish defender

"Ron's got as much character as a vintage Bentley."
John Gidman, who played under Ron at Old Trafford

"Our back four was at sixes and sevens."
After a poor defensive display

"I was in hospital with instructions not to have any visitors for 24 hours. I awoke to find Ron at the foot of the bed. 'Sorry I'm late,' he said, 'but I had to walk round the hospital three times before anybody recognised me'."
Broadcaster Gary Newbon

"What was the highlight of the tournament? 'Bumping into Frank Sinatra'."
Being quizzed on his impressions of the 1994 World Cup finals

"Ron is one of the top three managers in the game."
Doug Ellis, November 5th 1994

"It is with great regret that Aston Villa have decided to dispense with the services of Ron Atkinson."
Villa spokesman Abdul Rashid, November 9th 1994

— WE'RE FOREVER BLOWING DOUBLES —

When Villa won the League and FA Cup double in 1896/97 they became only the second club to achieve this after Preston North End in 1888 and no-one else managed it again until Spurs in 1960/61. However, there were several occasions when Villa came close to doing the double again themselves. In 1902/03 they finished second in the league, a point behind Sheffield Wednesday, and lost an FA Cup semi-final to eventual winners Bury. In 1912/13 they won the cup and were again runners-up in the league. The following season saw Villa reach the semi-final, and once more finish runners-up in the league.

— MURDER MOST FOUL —

There are many unique deeds associated with the Villa, but at least one of them is a distinction they would happily not lay claim to. In January 1924, the club became the only professional one in England ever to have a player murdered.

Thomas Ball was a wing-half from the north-east, who signed for Villa in January 1920, going on to replace the legendary Frank Barson in the first team. Ball and his wife Beatrice settled in Brick Kiln Lane, Perry Barr, where he fell out with his neighbour and landlord George Stagg, a First World War veteran. It was reckoned that the bone of contention between the two men grew when Ball began to keep chickens and a pet dog, who would regularly get into Stagg's garden.

On November 12th 1924, the Balls had spent the evening at the nearby Church Tavern, and returned home to find Stagg waiting for them. An argument broke out, and in the ensuing melee Stagg produced a firearm, subsequently described as either a rifle or his old service revolver, and shot Ball in the chest.

Ball fell to the ground and died almost immediately, at his wife's feet. Stagg was subsequently tried at Stafford Crown Court, claiming in his defence that Ball was drunk and that the gun had gone off by accident during a struggle. However, witnesses testified that Ball seemed in full control of his senses and that they had heard two shots. Furthermore, Stagg was an old soldier fully trained in the use of such weapons and when the judge could not get the gun to go off accidentally in court, the verdict became a formality. Stagg was convicted of murder and sentenced to hang, although this was later commuted to life imprisonment. Part of his clemency plea was that he had suffered a breakdown as a result of his wartime experiences.

Stagg was released from prison in 1945 and is believed to have died in a Birmingham mental hospital in 1966 aged 87. Nothing more was heard of Beatrice Ball after the trial. And when the Trinity Road stand was built in 1924, it contained what was reportedly the first players' bar in any English ground. Villa seemed keen to ensure that no more of their players ended up like Thomas Ball.

— THE FIRST HOLTE ENDER —

Of all Aston's previous inhabitants, none was as powerful as Sir Thomas Holte, builder of Aston Hall and mainstay of the family who owned the area for centuries.

Thomas Holte was born in 1571, at what was then the family's ancestral home, Duddeston Hall. Educated at Oxford, Holte was described as a learned man, versed in several languages, and gained a wide grasp of the law through time spent at the Inns of Court in London.

When Thomas was 21, his father died, and the young man used his contacts amongst the nobility to increase both the family's fortune and their influence. Knighted by James I as the new king made his way from Scotland to London to claim the throne in 1603, Holte remained in favour with his monarch and was able to buy a baronetcy eight years later. By now the highest-ranking amongst the local gentry, Holte decided that his new title deserved a fitting home, and so began the building of Aston Hall in 1616. Work was completed in 1635 and when it was finished, the hall was one of the finest Jacobean family homes in England, perched atop of a hill overlooking much of Sir Thomas's estates.

The Civil War that broke out in 1642 saw Holte in an uneasy position, his royalist sympathies making his lightly-fortified new home an obvious target for attack from the Parliamentarian stronghold of nearby Birmingham. King Charles I stayed at Aston Hall in October 1642, and the following December, the Hall came under attack from 1,200 Birmingham-based Parliamentarians, armed with a cannon. Holte was forced to surrender after a three-day siege during which 12 Cavaliers and 60 Roundheads were killed, and was imprisoned, his home plundered by the Parliamentarian forces.

Holte was a clever, shrewd and above all, ambitious man. He inherited much, and left even more, both in terms of wealth and also prestige. He retained the favour of successive monarchs, yet was also able to survive the Commonwealth of Oliver Cromwell without too much hardship. He was alleged to have murdered his cook in a violent rage, and although he sued for slander many years later over the incident, lost the case on appeal.

Sir Thomas Holte died in 1654, at the age of 83. He was married twice and had 16 children, outliving all but one daughter and was forced, reluctantly, to leave his estate to his grandson Robert, son of Edward, who Thomas had previously disinherited for marrying without his permission and who had died of plague whilst in the king's service during the civil war. Such was Thomas's displeasure at Edward's marriage that he resisted all pressure to be reunited with his son, even when asked to do so by King Charles.

Aston Hall, on whose grounds Villa Park now stands, stayed in the Holte family until 1817. It was then rented by James Watt Jnr, son of the great industrialist, and after a period of uncertainty sold to Birmingham Corporation in 1864.

— HALF-TIME READING —

The club's first matchday programme (*The Villa News and Record*) was published for the league game with Blackburn Rovers on September 1st 1906. By coincidence, Blackburn had been the first visitors to Villa Park, nine years earlier.

The programme contained 18 pages, and cost a penny. The front cover featured an advertisement for Rover Cycles, and William Shillcock had obviously been forgiven for losing the cup 11 years earlier (see *Ee Aye Addio We Lost The Cup*, page 30), as he was advertising his football boots and footballs, the latter used in the annual England v Scotland international and in several English Cup finals.

Edited by renowned journalist Mr WE Cox, the *News and Record* carried, along with team news and details of the afternoon's fixtures elsewhere, reports from the club's annual cricket match with Aston Unity and an account of the work being done by the Aston Villa & Theatrical Charity Sports Committee. There was also an article with regards to football finances. The previous season had seen Newcastle make the largest profit of any club in Britain, £4,399, whilst Villa's wage bill of £6,883 was higher than any other.

A reproduction was issued with the programme for Villa's centenary game, against Leeds United, on August 7th 1974.

— CATCHING THE 5.15. —

On 23rd September 1957 Villa lost to Wolves in a home first division game that kicked off at 5.15pm. The next time they kicked off at Villa Park at this odd hour was 5th February 2005, when they lost 3–1 to Arsenal. The former game kicked off at that time because Villa Park didn't yet possess floodlights; the latter was, inevitably, for television.

— GREAT VILLANS: THOMAS 'PONGO' WARING —

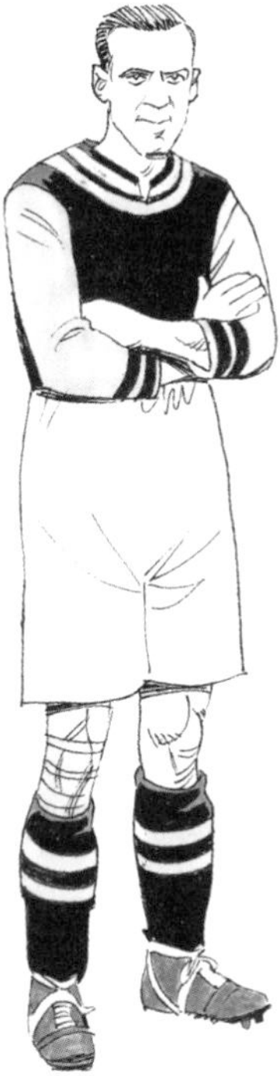

Pongo Waring: 171 goals for the Villa

Thomas Waring was born in October 1906, and made his professional debut for Tranmere Rovers. He caught the attention of the Villa, who dispatched directors Howard Spencer and John Devey on a scouting mission to watch the young forward, and their initial report stated that he was maybe worth a fee of £400. Waring's six goals against Durham City early in 1928 made them reassess their valuation and he was eventually signed for £4,700, then a record for a Third Division player, in November of that year.

Over six feet tall, Waring was a handful for any centre-half he tangled with, and unlike most target men of the era, he thought nothing of dropping deep to win the ball should service not be forthcoming. In this way, he was reminiscent of modern all-round strikers.

In 226 games for the Villa, Waring scored 171 goals, including a club record 49 in the 1930/31 season. Like many a Villa player before and since, Pongo was treated unfairly by the England set-up, playing just five internationals in which he scored four goals. It was reckoned that the main reason why Waring did not go on to play many times for his country was that his aggressive nature and uncertain temperament was too much for the FA to handle.

There were rumours, too, that his domestic circumstances hardly fell into the category of a happy home life. One story – which remains unconfirmed – is told of club secretary Billy Smith receiving a phone call one Monday morning from the governor of Winson Green prison, who said that he had Waring in one of his cells and, being a Villa supporter himself, didn't want to keep him. Smith replied that the Villa didn't particularly want the responsibility for their centre-forward either, and could the prison please look after Pongo, keep him fed, watered and out of trouble, then send him by taxi to Villa Park on Saturday morning together with a bill for his board and lodgings.

Waring was sold to Brighton in November 1935 and gradually wound down his career, making his final appearances for New Brighton FC during the war. It was at this time that he agreed to play in a reserve game at Villa Park in order that the Villa could take a look at a couple of youngsters he had recommended. Twenty thousand turned out to watch Waring make his last appearance in claret and blue and the kick-off had to be delayed in order to clear the pitch of youngsters seeking the great man's autograph.

There were several theories as to how Pongo received his nickname. In those more reverential times it was reckoned that he was named after a cartoon character. However, another story has it that Waring got the name because he embarked upon an England tour carrying just a toothbrush and no change of clothes, while Tranmere Rovers historian Gilbert Upton states that, "He earned the name because of his malodorous feet."

What is certain, though, is Pongo's last resting place. Dying in Birkenhead, in December 1980, his ashes were scattered in the

Holte End goalmouth prior to the Boxing Day game against Stoke City. There could have been no more fitting tribute to as good a centre-forward as ever played for the Villa.

— VILLA PARK II: WITTON LANE —

When Villa Park opened, Witton Lane housed the only seated accommodation in the ground. The stand had room for about 5,000 seated spectators, with a similar number housed on a lower terrace. The most remarkable feature of the stand was its triple-drum roof which was replaced in 1935 at a cost of £2,000, tip-up seats replacing the original benches two years later.

In 1943 the stand suffered considerable bomb damage, which was only repaired in 1954 after the club finally received permission from the Ministry of Works. Nine years later the old roof, the last surviving remnant of the original ground, was replaced by a much plainer, low, flat structure reflecting both the narrow space available to build on Witton Lane and the financial constraints under which the club were struggling at the time. The downstairs paddock was replaced by more seats in 1965 and apart from the introduction of 20 executive boxes during the eighties, Witton Lane stood, unloved and generally ignored, until the Taylor Report of 1990 meant that Villa Park needed to be modernised and ready for the abolition of terraces by the end of 1993/94.

The building of the new Witton Lane stand began at the end of the 1992/93 season and was managed entirely in-house, the first time a football club had embarked upon such a project, under the supervision of stadium manager Ted Small. Villa faced considerable opposition from local residents in their attempts to rebuild the ground and were often in conflict with the city council, who demanded that the club pay for the realignment of Witton Lane and the replacement of services that had been laid under the road. These demands boosted the costs of constructing the new stand to £5 million, of which £1.7 million was donated by the Football Trust. When the stand was fully opened, in January 1994, it held 5,500 in the lower tier, 4,686 upstairs and featured 36 executive boxes. Yet controversy never seemed far away.

Council planning regulations and the age-old problem of a

lack of space on Witton Lane meant that legroom was restricted downstairs and the upper concourse was narrower than the club would have liked. Of more worry for some supporters was the fact that they found themselves sitting in the Doug Ellis Stand, named as a birthday present to the Villa chairman three days after its opening. Doug claimed that the honour came as a complete surprise, and many people believed him. Finally, in the summer of 1995, remedial work to improve legroom led to the discovery of blue asbestos. As a result the club was fined under Health and Safety legislation, the lower tier of the stand was closed for several months and over 1,500 seats were lost.

— CHAMPIONS III: 1896/97 —

Villa's double-winning team established themselves as the pre-eminent side in the country, romping away with the title by a margin of eleven points. In contrast to the previous season, their results were better away from home than they were during what would prove to be the last games played at Perry Barr.

	P	W	D	L	F	A	Pts
Aston Villa	**30**	**21**	**5**	**4**	**73**	**38**	**47**
Sheffield United	30	13	10	7	42	29	36
Derby County	30	16	4	10	70	50	36
Preston North End	30	11	12	7	55	40	34
Liverpool	30	12	9	9	46	38	33
Sheffield Wednesday	30	10	11	9	42	37	31
Everton	30	14	3	13	62	57	31
Bolton Wanderers	30	12	6	12	40	43	30
Bury	30	10	10	10	39	44	30
Wolverhampton Wanderers	30	11	6	13	45	41	28
Nottingham Forest	30	9	8	13	44	49	26
West Bromwich Albion	30	10	6	14	33	56	26
Stoke	30	11	3	16	48	59	25
Blackburn Rovers	30	11	3	16	35	62	25
Sunderland	30	7	9	14	34	47	23
Burnley	30	6	7	17	43	61	19

— PRAWN SANDWICHES NOT INCLUDED —

When the consortium led by Doug Ellis took over in 1968 Villa were in deep financial trouble. This was hardly surprising when one considers that at the time, original shareholders in Aston Villa Ltd were still paying just 15/6d (77p) for two season tickets in the Trinity Road stand. 120 guests were also paying 5/3d (16p) a match for seats in the same stand, with tea and free car parking provided.

— NOTABLE VILLA APPEARANCES —

Once the season proper has ended, Villa have often provided the venue for many charitable games and local cup finals. During one week at the end of the 1984/85 season, two such matches gave supporters the opportunity to witness a couple of memorable, if fleeting, Villa Park appearances.

Doug Ellis's playing career is shrouded in mystery (see *Deadly's Varied Career*, page 18). He did, however, take the field in a charity game at Villa Park on May 12th 1985, coming on as a substitute for a Villa staff XI. During his five-minute appearance, Ellis touched the ball three times, and the opposition failed to dispossess him on any occasion. It's not known whether this was due to his mesmeric ball skills, or that they didn't want to risk harming a 61–year-old.

Five days later, Villa played West Brom in a fund-raising game for the victims of the Bradford fire. Appearing for Villa at the start of the game was George Best, who played 20 minutes and, a few days short of his 39th birthday, looked good enough to still be playing in the old First Division.

— FINAL COUNTDOWN 1 —

Celebrating the 1957 cup triumph

Villa have appeared in ten FA Cup finals, winning seven:

April 2nd 1887, Kennington Oval
Aston Villa 2 **West Bromwich Albion 0**
Hodgetts 20
Hunter 88

Villa: Warner, Coulton, Simmonds, Burton, Dawson, Yates, Davis, Brown, Hunter, Vaughton, Hodgetts

Albion: Roberts, H Green, Aldridge, Horton, Perry, Timmins, Woodall, T Green, Bayliss, Pearson, Paddock
Att: 15,500

March 19th 1892, Kennington Oval
Aston Villa 0 **West Bromwich Albion 3**
Pearson 5
Nicholls 30
Reynolds 55

Villa: Warner, Evans, Cox, H Devey, Cowan, Baird, Athersmith, J Devey, Dixon, Hodgetts, Campbell

Albion: Reader, Nicholson, McCullock, Reynolds, Perry, Groves, Bassett, McLeod, Nicholls, Pearson, Geddes
Att: 32,810

April 20th 1895, Crystal Palace
Aston Villa 1 **West Bromwich Albion 0**
Devey 1

Villa: Wilkes, Spencer, Welford, Reynolds, Cowan, Russell, Athersmith, Chatt, Devey, Hodgetts, Smith

Albion: Reader, Horton, Williams, Perry, Higgins, Taggart, Bassett, McLeod, Richards, Hutchinson, Banks
Att: 42,652

April 10th 1897, Crystal Palace
Aston Villa 3 **Everton 2**
Campbell 18 Bell 23
Wheldon 39 Boyle 29
Crabtree 44

Villa: Whitehouse, Spencer, Reynolds, James Cowan, Crabtree, Athersmith, Devey, Campbell, Wheldon, John Cowan

Everton: Menham, Meecham, Storrier, Boyle, Holt, Stewart, Taylor, Bell, Hartley, Chadwick, Millward
Att: 65,024

April 15th 1905, Crystal Palace
Aston Villa 2 **Newcastle United 0**
Hampton 3, 75

Villa: George, Spencer, Miles, Pearson, Lake, Windmill, Brawn, Garratty, Hampton, Bache, Hall

Newcastle: Lawrence, McCombie, Carr, Gardner, Aitken, McWilliam, Rutherford, Howie, Appleyard, Veitch, Gosnell
Att: 101,000

April 19th 1913, Crystal Palace
Aston Villa 1 **Sunderland 0**
Barber 83

Villa: Hardy, Lyons, Weston, Barber, Harrop, Leach, Wallace, Halse, Hampton, Stephenson, Bache

Sunderland: Butler, Gladwin, Ness, Cuggy, Thomson, Low, Mordue, Buchan, Richardson, Holley, Martin
Att: 120,081 (this is the biggest crowd ever to watch the Villa).

April 24th 1920, Stamford Bridge
Aston Villa 1 **Huddersfield Town 0 (aet)**
Kirton 97

Villa: Hardy, Smart, Weston, Ducat, Barson, Moss, Wallace, Kirton, Walker, Stephenson, Dorrell

Huddersfield: Mutch, Wood, Bullock, Slade, Wilson, Watson, Richardson, Mann, Taylor, Swan, Islip
Att: 50,000

April 26th 1924, Wembley
Aston Villa 0 **Newcastle United 2**
Cowan 85
Seymour 87

Villa: Jackson, Smart, Mort, Moss, Milne, Blackburn, York, Kirton, Capewell, Walker, Dorrell

Newcastle: Bradley, Hampson, Hudspeth, Mooney, Spencer, Gibson, Low, Cowan, McDonald, Harris, Seymour
Att: 91,695

May 4th 1957, Wembley
Aston Villa 2 **Manchester United 1**
McParland 67, 72 Taylor 84

Villa: Sims, Lynn, Aldis, Crowther, Dugdale, Saward, Smith, Sewell, Myerscough, Dixon, McParland

Man Utd: Wood, Foulkes, Byrne, Colman, Blanchflower, Edwards, Berry, Whelan, Taylor, Charlton, Pegg
Att: 100,000

May 20th 2000, Wembley

Aston Villa 0	**Chelsea 1**
	Di Matteo 73

Villa: James, Delaney, Ehiogu, Southgate, Barry, Wright (Hendrie), Boateng, Merson, Taylor (Stone), Carbone (Joachim), Dublin

Chelsea: De Goey, Melchiot, Desailly, Leboeuf, Babayaro, Poyet, Wise, Deschamps, Di Matteo, Zola (Morris), Weah (Flo)
Att: 78,217

— GREAT GAMES 3: 'A TRULY OLYMPIAN STRUGGLE' —

Aston Villa 3	**Everton 2**
Campbell	Bell
Wheldon	Boyle
Crabtree	

April 10th 1897: FA Cup Final
Att: 65,024

1897 saw Villa win through to the FA Cup final for the fourth time. Their opponents were Everton and the game attracted a crowd of 65,024, of whom a third were reckoned to be Villa supporters, taking advantage of a special Birmingham Works holiday granted for the occasion. They were to witness a game generally regarded as the finest cup final of the Victorian era.

The game began at a cracking pace and Villa dominated the midfield for the first 15 minutes. The left side pairing of John Devey and Charlie Athersmith stretched the Everton defence and after 18 minutes Villa went ahead with a goal by centre-forward John Campbell. Villa tried to press their advantage, but conceded an equaliser five minutes later and went 2–1 down just before the half-hour mark, both goals coming as a result of fast Everton breaks out of defence.

However, wing-half Jimmy Crabtree's free-kick found inside-right Fred Wheldon after 40 minutes and Villa were level. Supporters were already delighted with what they had seen, but the Villa elements of the crowd were further cheered when, shortly before half-time, Crabtree headed Villa's third and, as it turned out, winning, goal.

Whereas Villa's forwards had dominated the first half, so Everton had most of the play after the break. But they could not get past a Villa defence with full-backs Howard Spencer and Albert Evans outstanding while at the other end Campbell and Devey both went close.

The game ended with the Villa team having achieved a feat that will surely remain unique in football history. Since a full league programme took place on cup final day back in those times and with results having gone their way, Villa were crowned league champions on the same day they won the FA Cup.

Lord Roseberry presented Villa captain John Devey with the FA Cup trophy they had bought themselves to replace the one stolen two years earlier, paying tribute to the Villa's performance with the words, "I can judge the great qualities that both sides have displayed – these qualities we recognize as distinctly British. It was truly a great Olympian struggle."

— ALL CHANGE —

There was a time when many supporters would watch Villa one week and Birmingham City the next. They could have been excused for being confused on 14th February 1953, when Blues played Chelsea in the FA Cup fifth round wearing claret and blue while Villa won 3–1 at Rotherham in blue. Under the rules of the FA Cup at the time, both teams were required to change when colours clashed: if their change shirts also clashed one or both teams would borrow a set from another club. Villa borrowed a set of Blues strips on several occasions, the last time coming in a sixth round replay in March 1957, when they wore Birmingham's red and white change colours in a 2–0 win over Burnley.

— CHAMPIONS IV: 1898/99 —

Villa's fourth championship success was the most dramatic of the lot. On the final day of the season they were due to play Liverpool, who were second in the table level on points but with an inferior goal difference. The trophy was present at Villa Park to be presented to the winners, and despite Villa needing just a point to be crowned champions they attacked from the off, going in at half-time 5–0 up. Although there were no further goals in the second half, Villa had clinched the title in some style.

	P	W	D	L	F	A	Pts
Aston Villa	**34**	**19**	7	8	**76**	**40**	**45**
Liverpool	34	19	5	10	49	33	43
Burnley	34	15	9	10	45	47	39
Everton	34	15	8	11	48	41	38
Notts County	34	12	13	9	47	51	37
Blackburn Rovers	34	14	8	12	60	52	36
Sunderland	34	15	6	13	41	41	36
Wolverhampton Wanderers	34	14	7	13	54	48	35
Derby County	34	12	11	11	62	57	35
Bury	34	14	7	13	48	49	35
Nottingham Forest	34	11	11	12	42	42	33
Stoke	34	13	7	14	47	52	33
Newcastle United	34	11	8	15	49	48	30
West Bromwich Albion	34	12	6	16	42	57	30
Preston North End	34	10	9	15	44	47	29
Sheffield United	34	9	11	14	45	51	29
Bolton Wanderers	34	9	7	18	37	51	25
Sheffield Wednesday	34	8	8	18	32	61	24

— GREAT VILLANS: BRIAN LITTLE —

A symbol of Villa's climb back from the abyss

His goalscoring record was hardly the best, he sometimes drifted through games looking disinterested and he once went almost a year without scoring, yet Brian Little remains one of the most popular post-war Villa players and even to this day grown men become misty-eyed at the mere mention of his name. The reasons are obvious to anyone who witnessed Little's career – not only was he capable of moments of sublime skill, but he was also symbolic of Villa's climb back from the abyss.

Born in Newcastle upon Tyne in 1953, Little joined Villa straight from school and became the first star graduate of the club's revived youth policy. He made his first-team debut towards the end of the 1971/72 season, scoring against Torquay, and played in the FA Youth Cup-winning team alongside his brother Alan and fellow future England international John Gidman.

Little went on to become a regular in the Villa side, and his 24 goals in the League Cup and promotion double season of 1974/75 led to an England debut when he made a ten-minute substitute appearance in the Home International versus Wales (Villa's first England cap since Gerry Hitchens). Despite this promising start Little was never selected for the national side again and his international career remains one of the shortest on record.

1976/77 saw Little's finest moment. A hat-trick in the League Cup semi-final replay with QPR was followed by two goals in the second replay of the final against Everton, as Villa won the trophy for the third time. In total, Little scored 26 goals that season.

The next three years saw Little struggling to recapture his form, and a knee injury sustained against Wolves in March 1980 was to lead to him announcing his retirement from football in 1981, with Villa on the verge of their greatest modern-day triumphs. In total he had played 306 games and scored 82 goals.

Little remained at Villa Park, working first in the club's commercial department then as youth team coach, before falling out with manager Graham Turner and spending time as Wolves manager and then on the coaching staff at Middlesbrough. Little returned to management with Darlington, leading them from the Conference to the Third Division in successive years, before joining Leicester, who he eventually guided to the Premier League in 1994.

When Ron Atkinson was sacked as Villa manager later that year Little took up his inevitable position as Aston Villa manager, the appointment being made on his 41st birthday. After an initial struggle, Little's team thrived under the 3-5-2 formation he employed to good effect. 1995/96 saw a fourth place in the Premiership and the Coca-Cola Cup won. Fifth place in the league the following season led to Villa being tipped as a good bet for the title, but several inopportune signings, in particular Sasa Curcic and Stan Collymore, saw the team struggling and Little resigned as Villa manager in February 1998.

Periods in charge of Stoke, Albion, Hull and Tranmere saw periods of initial success and then decline, while recent years have seen him managing Wrexham and Gainsborough Trinity, of the Northern Premier League. It's difficult to argue with the assessment that Brian Little's heart has never truly been in the game since he left Villa.

— HAT-TRICK EURO-HEROES —

Three players have scored hat-tricks for the Villa in European competition:

Player	Date	Comp	Result
Gary Shaw	Nov 3rd 1982	European Cup	Villa 4 Din. Bucharest 2
Peter Withe	Sept 28th 1983	UEFA Cup	Villa 5 Vitoria Guimares 0
Stan Collymore	Sept 29th 1998	UEFA Cup	Stromsgodset 0 Villa 3

— MERRY CHRISTMAS —

There was a time when Football League fixtures were arranged so that clubs would play each other home and away over the Christmas period. With uncertain weather, heavy pitches and the amount of travelling involved, results would often be unpredictable with a heavy defeat frequently followed within a day or two by an even more convincing victory. The practice, which from Villa's point of view began in 1907/08, with a 4–0 home defeat by Nottingham Forest on Christmas Day followed by a 2–2 draw at the City Ground on Boxing Day, was a regular feature of football between the wars, and gradually petered out by the mid-sixties.

Notable examples included:

1914/15	December 26th	Villa 1 Bolton Wanderers 7
	January 1st	Bolton Wanderers 2 Villa 2
1920/21	December 25th	Villa 3 Manchester United 4
	December 27th	Manchester United 1 Villa 3
1924/25	December 25th	Leeds United 6 Villa 0
	December 26th	Villa 2 Leeds United 1
1931/32	December 25th	Villa 7 Middlesbrough 1
	December 26th	Middlesbrough 1 Villa 1
1932/33	December 26th	Villa 1 Wolves 3
	December 27th	Wolves 2 Villa 4
1933/34	December 25th	Villa 6 Wolves 2
	December 26th	Wolves 4 Villa 3

1935/36	December 25th December 26th	Villa 4 Huddersfield Town 1 Huddersfield Town 1 Villa 4
1938/39	December 25th December 26th	Sunderland 1 Villa 5 Villa 1 Sunderland 1
1948/49	December 25th December 27th	Wolves 4 Villa 0 Villa 5 Wolves 1
1949/50	December 26th December 27th	Wolves 2 Villa 3 Villa 1 Wolves 4

The last double-header was in 1966/67, when Villa lost 2–1 away at Sunderland on Boxing Day, then won the return match by the same score the following day. Ironically, Sunderland had also been Villa's last Christmas Day opponents, beating Villa 1–0 at Roker Park on December 25th 1956.

— A WORD FROM OUR SPONSORS —

The first sponsor's name to appear on a Villa shirt was Barratt Homes, for Brian Little's testimonial in April 1982. The next season local brewers Davenport's became Villa's first regular shirt sponsors.

The full list of Villa shirt sponsors is:

1982–83: Davenport's brewers
1982–93: Mita/Mita Copiers, photocopier manufacturers
1993–95: Muller, yogurt makers
1995–98: AST, computer hardware company
1998–2000: LDV Vans
2000–02: NTL, communications company
2002–04: Rover, car manufacturer
2004–06: DWS, investment bankers
2006–07: 32Red, online gambling company
2008–10: Sponsorship was donated to the Acorns Children's Hospice
2010–11: FX Pro, online foreign exchange dealers
2011– : Genting, casino owners.

In June 2008 Villa announced that the club would be donating its shirt sponsorship for the 2008/09 season to the Acorns Children's Hospice.

— KIT DESIGNERS —

Since these things began to matter, Villa's kits have been made by:

1974–81 – Umbro
1981–85 – Le Coq Sportif
1985–87 – Henson
1987–90 – Hummel
1990–93 – Umbro
1993–95 – Asics
1995–2000 – Reebok
2000–04 – Diadora
2004–07 – Hummel
2007–12 – Nike

From the start of the 2012/13 season Villa's kit will be designed by Macron.

— YOUNG AT HEART —

Villa can claim to have the longest-running retired players' team in the world. In the 1880s a side comprising former Villa stars, including Archie Hunter, the club's first great name, would play matches against local opposition to raise money for hospital beds and other community needs.

In the 1960s the Aston Villa Old Stars was formally constituted, and to date have raised around £3 million for charity. They currently play around 25 matches every year and legendary names from the past such as Nigel Spink, Gordon Cowans and Tony Morley are regulars in the side, alongside newer names like Ian Taylor and Mark Kinsella.

Running alongside the Old Stars is the Aston Villa Former Players' Association, launched in 1995 to help raise funds for ex-Villa players in need. Under the chairmanship of former defender Neil Rioch, the FPA is widely regarded as the best-run former players' organisation in the game.

— PLAYERS OF THE YEAR —

Surprisingly, no Villa player has ever won the Player of the Year award voted for by the Football Writers' Association. However, the club has achieved more success in the PFA awards. The roll of honour here consists of:

Player of the Year
1977: Andy Gray
1990: David Platt
1993: Paul McGrath

Young Player of the Year
1977: Andy Gray
1981: Gary Shaw

Andy Gray was the first player to win Player of the Year and Young Player of the Year in the same season. His achievement was matched by Cristiano Ronaldo in 2007.

— ONE GAME WONDERS —

Sixty-one players have made just one official appearance for the Villa first team. Of these, six unfortunates – Frank Bedingfield (1898/99), George A. Davis (1892/93), Jim Garfield (1899/1900), Tommy Moore (1931/32), Tom Purslow (1894/95) and David Skea (1892/93) – scored.

Other notable single appearance-makers include Ralph Brown, whose sole game was in the League Cup final first leg against Rotherham in 1961 and Arthur Proudler, who made his debut in November 1954 against Leicester City. Proudler was promptly knocked out in an accidental collision with a team-mate after ten minutes, spent much of the first-half being treated and then re-emerged onto the pitch (this was in the days before substitutes) barely able to walk.

— GREAT VILLANS: CHARLIE ATHERSMITH —

Charlie Athersmith was probably Villa's best-known player of the late Victorian era, and widely regarded at the time as the finest outside-right in the world. Born in 1872, Athersmith began his career with his home-town club, Bloxwich Wanderers, reputedly playing in their senior team at the age of eleven. His footballing skills began to attract attention and, after a spell with Saltley Unity Gas, he signed as a professional for the Villa in January

1891, making his league debut two months later aged 19, against Preston North End.

From then on, Athersmith was a first-team regular for the rest of his Villa career, and so fast was his rise to prominence that by the end of 1891/92, his first full league campaign, he had already been capped for England.

In the 1896/97 season, he won FA Cup and Football League winners medals, played in every England international – against Scotland, Wales and Ireland – as well as turning out for the Football League against the Scottish League. In doing so, he gained every honour available to an English footballer in a given season. This was the only time such a feat was achieved.

Athersmith was two-footed, and with an armoury of tricks second to none he could beat an opponent either with sheer speed, or in the unlikely event that the other side's full-back could match the Villa winger's blistering pace, Athersmith's ball control would invariably be employed to leave his opposite number stranded. Charlie would then place a pin-point cross onto his centre-forward's head or else deliver the ball with deadly accuracy to his inside-right.

A natural athlete, Athersmith was regarded as one of the fastest quarter-milers in the Midlands, and in his youth there was speculation that he would spurn a footballing career in order to concentrate on his running. Fortunately for the Villa, Charlie decided that he preferred sprinting down the right wing to around a track, and he remained a favourite of the crowds until the summer of 1901, when the Villa committee decided that his best days were behind him. Even the greatest of players were considered surplus to requirements by George Ramsay & Co once they were believed to be past their best and Athersmith moved to Small Heath, for whom he made over 100 senior appearances.

Like many former players, Charlie found life outside football difficult and lost much of his wealth in failed business ventures. He died suddenly at his mother's house in Oakengates, Shropshire, on September 18th 1910. It was thought that his premature death was caused by a kick to the stomach suffered many years earlier, during his playing days, and which had caused more damage than was originally thought.

— LOYAL SERVANTS —

Villa's top ten highest appearances makers:

Charlie Aitken	660
Billy Walker	531
Gordon Cowans	527
Allan Evans	476
Joe Bache	474
Nigel Spink	460
Tommy Smart	452
Johnny Dixon	430
Dennis Mortimer	406
Billy George	402

— PROLIFIC MARKSMEN —

Villa's ten highest goalscorers:

Billy Walker	244
Harry Hampton	242
John Devey	187
Eric Houghton	185
Joe Bache	170
Tom Waring	167
Johnny Dixon	144
Peter McParland	120
Dai Astley	100
Len Capewell	100

— HAPPY FAMILIES —

There have been several examples of members of the same family playing for the Villa. These include:

Brothers:

Albert A. (1884) and Arthur (1878–79, 80–86) Brown
Chris (1906–14) and Frank (1903–05) Buckley
James (1889–1902) and John (1895–1899) Cowan
Arthur, Harry (1877–93), John (1891–1902) and William (1892–94) Devey. Their brother Arthur was also on Villa's books without playing for the first team.
George (1914–15) and Harry (1904–20) Hampton
George (1934–38) and Sam (1912–21) Hardy
Andy (1879–94) and Archie (1878–90) Hunter
Alan (1971–74) and Brian (1969–81) Little
Alec (1907–09) and James Lochhead (1905–12) Logan
Bert (1913–14) and John (1912–15) McLachlan
Tom (1882–83) and Billy (1874–80) Mason
Luke (2002–) and Stefan (1999–2005) Moore
Bruce (1969–74) and Neil (1969–75) Rioch
Bert (1897–99) and John (1897–99) Sharp
Henry (1878–90) and Joe (1882–87) Simmonds
Clem (1910–21), George T (1919–27) and James (1914–21) Stephenson
Ernie (1899–1901) and Walter M (1904) Watkins

Father and son(s):

William (1894–96) and Arthur (1919–1931) Dorrell
Frank Snr (1914–29), Amos (1939–56) and Frank Jnr (1938–55) Moss

Grandfather and grandson:

Isaac (1889–90) and Thomas (1932–34) Moore

Uncle and nephew:

Cecil Harris (1922–26) and Eric Houghton (1927–46)
John (1895–97) and Archibald (1922–25) Campbell

— GREAT VILLANS: PETER WITHE —

Peter Withe scores one of his more important goals for Villa in 1982

Peter Withe was, in footballing terms, the classic late developer. Born in August 1951, Withe's career began as he was working as an electrician on Liverpool docks, when he signed for non-league Skelmersdale. Withe first turned professional with Southport, then spent time with Barrow before moving to South Africa, where he played for Port Elizabeth and Arcadia Shepherds.

On his return to England, Withe signed for Wolves, then Birmingham City, before moving to Nottingham Forest in the summer of 1976. Never did a player join a club at a better time, because under Brian Clough, unheralded Forest gained promotion to the First Division, then won the league championship and League Cup in 1977/78. With Garry Birtles making his way into the team, Withe was surplus to requirements and he was sold to Second Division Newcastle United, where he spent two unremarkable seasons before Ron Saunders, looking for a centre-forward to replace Andy Gray, paid what was then a club record fee of £500,000 in June 1980.

Most observers thought this to be a mistake. Withe was 28, had spent almost all his career in the lower divisions and was generally regarded as over the hill. Saunders proved himself to be a much better judge of a footballer than 'most observers' because Withe and Gary Shaw formed the finest strike partnership Villa supporters had seen for decades. In his first season at Villa Park, Withe scored 21 goals and was instrumental in helping Villa to win the First Division championship. He was also the only Villa player that year to win full international honours, making his

England debut against Brazil at Wembley. In all, Withe played 11 times for England, scoring one goal.

The following year saw Withe score the greatest goal in the club's history, the famous mis-hit from Tony Morley's cross that hit his shin and bobbled into the Bayern Munich goal in the European Cup final. Two seasons later came Withe's most productive season for the Villa, when he scored 22 goals.

In total, Withe played 253 games for the Villa, scoring 92 goals. Signed as a target man, there was always more to his game than mere physical presence and aerial ability. Withe was an under-rated all-rounder, skilful and better at holding up the ball than any other English forward of his era. Such talent led Brian Clough to say, "My biggest mistake was selling Peter Withe. My second-biggest was not buying him back."

Withe was regarded as the hardest-training player at the club, and invariably the last player to leave Bodymoor Heath every day. Supporters loved him for his never-say-die attitude, which led to regular trouble with officials, as he tended to regard the referee's whistle as an opening of negotiations rather than a final decision.

Withe left Villa for Sheffield United in 1985, then spent a while as player-coach with Huddersfield Town, returning to Villa Park in January 1991, first as assistant manager to Joszef Venglos then reserve team coach under Ron Atkinson. After an unhappy spell as manager of Wimbledon, Withe became Villa's head of European scouting for a time before moving to the Far East to coach first the Thai and then the Indonesian national sides. In the summer of 2012 Peter returned to the UK to manage Evo-Stick Northern League side Woodley Sports.

— THROUGHOUT THE CENTURIES —

If you really want to scrape the bottom of the barrel of notable Villa achievements it could be claimed that the 5–2 aggregate win over FC Basle in the Intertoto Cup final of 2001 meant they were the first English club to win a trophy in three different centuries.

— HALL OF FAME —

In 2007 a poll was conducted on the official Villa website to find the first 12 members of the Aston Villa Hall of Fame. Incumbents were as follows:

William McGregor (committee member/life member 1881–1911)
George Ramsay (player 1876–82, club secretary 1884–1926)
Eric Houghton (player 1929–47, manager 1953–58, director 1972–79)
Trevor Ford (player 1946–51)
Peter McParland (player 1952–62)
Charlie Aitken (player 1959–76)
Brian Little (player 1969–81, manager 1994–98)
Ron Saunders (manager 1974–82)
Peter Withe (player 1980–85)
Dennis Mortimer (player1975–85)
Gordon Cowans (player 1974–85, 1988–92, 1993–94)
Paul McGrath (player 1989–96)

— A LEAGUE CUP FIRST —

The inaugural League Cup competition, held in 1960/61, was one of the strangest trophy wins the Villa have ever known. The cup was derided from its inception, known as 'Hardaker's Folly' after its originator Alan Hardaker, then-secretary of the Football League, and shunned by many First Division clubs.

The competition itself was played over two different seasons. Due to fixture congestion the final could not be played before the end of the season, and was therefore held over until 1961/62 was underway. Villa's opponents were Rotherham United, who won the first leg, played at their Millmoor ground, 2–0 on August 22nd 1961. The second leg took place on September 5th. Villa won 3–0 after extra-time to claim the trophy 3–2 on aggregate. Ralph Brown made his only senior appearance in the first leg, while the return took place just eight days before Villa's first defence of the trophy, a 4–3 victory away at Bradford City.

— SOME PEOPLE ON THE PITCH —

Villa Park has often been used for major events other than football matches. However, not all of these occasions have passed off smoothly.

- Coventry's Danny McAlinden fought Jack Bodell of Derbyshire for the British heavyweight title on the Villa Park pitch in June 1972. So many of McAlinden's fans invaded the ring after his third-round victory that their combined weight caused the structure to collapse.
- In May 1975 Barry White played a concert at Villa Park. Ticket sales were poor and the promoters took 12 months to clear the debts they incurred.
- The next concert to take place at Villa Park featured local heroes Duran Duran in July 1983. Although the organisation was faultless the concert, in aid of mental health charity MENCAP, sold fewer tickets than expected and little money was raised.
- A rally by evangelist Billy Graham in May 1984 drew the biggest crowd that has ever been attracted to a Villa Park event, over a quarter of a million people attending over the course of a week. However, an inspection by council officials revealed that fire exits were locked during the events and the club was subsequently fined by local magistrates.
- Bruce Springsteen played two dates at Villa Park in June 1988. These were well-attended and everything passed off peacefully. However, freak atmospherics meant that the show could be heard a reported 20 miles away and led to a string of complaints.
- As a result, there were protests from local residents prior to the Rod Stewart concert that took place in July 1995. Stewart didn't help matters by saying that they should go to the beach for the day and concert-goers arrived in Aston to see local people sunbathing on a pile of sand they had brought in for the occasion. The concert passed without any other incident.

— GREAT VILLANS: CHARLIE AITKEN —

Charlie Aitken: First choice for 16 seasons

Born in Edinburgh in 1942, Charlie joined Villa straight from school. He made his first team debut in 1961, in the victory over Sheffield Wednesday that also marked Johnny Dixon's last game for the club, and was Villa's first-choice left-back for an astonishing 16 seasons. As one of the Mercer Minors, the talented collection of youngsters that came to fruition under the management of Joe Mercer, Charlie played alongside such fledgling stars as Alan Deakin and Harry Burrows. Yet a combination of ill-luck, injury and mismanagement meant that they, and the team as a whole, failed to fulfil their potential. The team that many had tipped to dominate English football during the sixties ended up relegated from the First Division in 1967.

Aitken could have been forgiven for wanting to leave several times during his Villa career, as this period encompassed the team's lowest ebb. But Aitken was strictly a one-club man and his loyalty was partly rewarded by a League Cup winner's medal in 1975 and the knowledge that he had played his part in helping Villa on their first steps to recovery.

Aitken's greatest asset was his remarkable level of fitness. Not only was he the quickest man on the Villa's books for many years, he was also able to shrug off injuries that would have sidelined a lesser man. He first arrived in the Villa team when tactical thinking was a rarity and a manager's instructions to his full-backs had scarcely changed in the previous half-century – mark the wingers and get rid of the ball as soon as possible. By the time he left the Villa, wingers were becoming extinct and full-backs were often their team's prime source of attacking inspiration.

In 1974, Aitken passed Billy Walker's long-standing record of 478 league appearances for the Villa and was presented with a commemorative plaque by Walker's widow prior to the game. Aitken went on to play in a total of 656 first-team games, 559 of them in the league, and score 16 goals.

The arrival of Ron Saunders and subsequent promotion back to the First Division meant that Aitken's days at Villa Park were numbered, and he was given a free transfer at the end of the 1975/76 season. The following year, he was granted a rare second testimonial, against a Midlands Select XI. It was said of Aitken that the only thing remaining unchanged at Villa Park during his Villa career was the old grass bank at the Witton End. Not long after his departure, plans were revealed for the demolition of this last remaining original feature of the ground where Villa had first played in 1897.

Like many other players of the time, Aitken moved to the North American Soccer League, where he spent two years playing for the New York Cosmos, alongside Pele, Franz Beckenbauer and Carlos Alberto before finally hanging up his boots in 1977.

Aitken moved back to Birmingham after his time in America and later became a vice-president of the Villa. He is now honorary chairman of the Former Players' Association.

— BODYMOOR HEATH —

Villa's training ground to the north east of Birmingham originally cost £65,000 and was situated on twenty acres of land bought from a local farmer. It was opened in December 1971 and at the time was considered the most modern facility of its type in the country. However, over the years the training ground became increasingly outdated, to the frustration of more than one Villa manager. For John Gregory the state of Bodymoor Heath was one of the reasons why he described Doug Ellis as "living in a timewarp" in a *Sunday Times* interview of 2000. Three years later Graham Taylor stated that when he returned as manager Bodymoor was "nowhere near good enough. We had to spend £350,000 just to get the surfaces right."

As Ellis became increasingly cost-conscious, Bodymoor was often the victim of his economy drives. In November 2005 an £8 million redevelopment was announced, only to be scrapped within months due to concern over the club's finances. This decision was one of the reasons behind the statement leaked to the press by senior players the following summer criticising the club's lack of ambition.

Following Randy Lerner's takeover in September 2006, the Bodymoor redevelopment was once more revived and the new facilities were opened by club captain Gareth Barry and former captain Dennis Mortimer in May 2007.

The project cost over £12 million and was designed to make Bodymoor Heath once again the best training facility in English football. The ground floor of the two-storey building contains offices for the chairman, secretary and manager, plus the players' welfare officer, the coaching staff and Academy staff. In addition to dressing rooms for every level of the club's players from under-nines to the first team, the complex boasts a sauna and steam rooms, a swimming pool, hot and cold plunge pools and a hydro-therapy pool to assist recovery from injuries.

Adjoining the main building is an indoor arena which includes a 70m running track, while a further £2.8 million was spent on pitches, one of which is an exact replica of the Villa Park surface, right down to the size, type of grass and camber.

— VILLA AT THE WORLD CUP —

Peter Withe was the first Villa player to be selected for an England World Cup finals squad, although he failed to make any appearances in 1982. Four years later, Steve Hodge played in all five England games. David Platt then made six appearances during Italia 90, scoring three goals. In 1998, Gareth Southgate played in two of England's four games. Finally, Darius Vassell played three times for England in the 2002 finals.
Other Villa players selected for World Cup squads are:

1958 Peter McParland (Northern Ireland)
1982 Allan Evans (Scotland)
1990 Tony Cascarino, Paul McGrath (Republic of Ireland)
1994 Ray Houghton, Paul McGrath, Andy Townsend, Steve Staunton (Republic of Ireland)
1998 Savo Milosevic (FR Yugoslavia)
2002 Alpay Ozalan (Turkey), Steve Staunton (Republic of Ireland) Olof Mellberg (Sweden) Bosko Balaban (Croatia)
2006 Ulises de la Cruz (Ecuador) Milan Baros (Czech Republic), Olof Mellberg (Sweden)
2010 Emile Heskey, James Milner, Stephen Warnock (England)

— HOT SHOT SCHMEICHEL —

Peter Schemeichel's Villa career will never be talked about in the same breath as his time with Manchester United. However, while he was with Villa Schemeichel performed at least one feat he never achieved at Old Trafford. On October 20th 2001, with Villa trailing 3–1 to Everton, Schmeichel went upfield for a last-minute corner and hooked home a loose ball to become the first goalkeeper to score in the Premier League as well as the only Villa keeper to achieve such a feat in a competitive match. Sadly, his efforts were in vain as there was no further score in the remainder of the game and Villa lost 3–2.

— THE SUPREME SACRIFICE —

Football continued as normal after the First World War broke out in August 1914. Most people believed the war would be over in a matter of weeks, so the 1914/15 season was allowed to carry on. However, during the summer of 1915 it became clear that there would be no quick end to the conflict and footballers were criticised for continuing to play while their countrymen were being slaughtered.

The league and cup programme was subsequently cancelled for the duration of the war and many players volunteered for the armed forces. A Footballers' Battalion was formed in the army and several Villa players served with distinction. Of these, Arthur Dobson was the only fatality although three former Villa players, Alfred Edwards, Billy Gerrish and Walter Kimberley, were also killed in action.

— MOTORING AWAY —

Modern footballers drive Bentleys, high-performance 4x4s and whichever Italian sports cars are in fashion this week. In the seventies though, Villa players had very different wheels:

Brian Little: MGB GT
Frank Carrodus: BMW 316
Jim Cumbes: Ford Cortina
Jimmy Brown: Ford Capri
Leighton Phillips: Vauxhall Cavalier
Sammy Morgan: Triumph Spitfire
Mick Wright: Ford Cortina
Charlie Aitken: Lotus Cortina
John Deehan: Triumph TR7
Chico Hamilton: Ford Capri
Fred Turnbull: Vauxhall Victor

In 1977 the club did a deal with a local car showroom that meant the players could have any car of their choice – up to the value of £4,000.

— WHAT A WASTE OF MONEY! —

Some of Villa's most inexplicable signings:

Ivo Stas: Signed by Jo Venglos for £250,000 in 1990, after playing for Banik Ostrava against Villa in the UEFA Cup (and scoring an own goal). Injured in his first training session and never played a first-team game, before being forced to retire in 1992.

Bosko Balaban: Signed from Dinamo Zagreb in the summer of 2001 for £5.6 million. Despite spending so much money on him, John Gregory steadfastly refused to pick Balaban for the first team, restricting his appearances to one start in the League Cup, another in the UEFA Cup (both ties were lost) and a handful of substitute appearances. Graham Taylor loaned Balaban back to Dinamo, who returned him after a year. David O'Leary then cancelled his contract in December 2003 and he joined Bruges. Three managers, no league starts, no goals.

John Fashanu: Signed for £1.35 million by Ron Atkinson in the summer of 1994. He'd already stated that he was looking to wind down his football career and was moving into television. 13 appearances, three goals and an innocuous-looking challenge from Ryan Giggs in a league game at Old Trafford led to Fashanu's hastily-announced retirement.

Stan Collymore: Cost a club record £7 million from Liverpool in 1997. Regarded as the final piece in the jigsaw, Stan behaved more like the missing link. Breakdowns, assaults, disappearances, sendings-off and just seven goals in 46 games.

Fabio Ferraresi: Signed from Serie C1 club Cesena on a free transfer in 1998. His time at Villa was limited to a brief appearance as substitute in a UEFA Cup tie and a few reserve team games. Sent back from whence he came the following summer, Ferraresi's Villa career is notable only for the fact that a story later emerged of how he was allegedly signed in the belief Villa were getting Cagliari midfielder Enzo Maresca, who moved to Albion at the same time and was eventually sold to Juventus for £4.3 million.

— GREAT GAMES 4: EIGHT, NINE, TEN —

Aston Villa 6	**Blackburn Rovers 4**
Warnock,	Kalinic (2)
Milner,	Olsson,
Dunne,	Emerton
Agbonlahor,	
Heskey,	
Young	

20th January 2010 Carling Cup semi-final second leg
Villa Park. Att: 40,604

Villa have saved some of their most memorable occasions for the League Cup, and rarely have they achieved success the easy way. But never has there been a game like the one which saw the club into their eighth appearance in the final of the competition. It seemed straightforward at kick-off – a James Milner goal in the first leg at Ewood Park had given them a lead which should have been enough to see Villa through to Wembley without any problems. A goalless draw would have been enough. Rovers, though, had other ideas and took just ten minutes to level the aggregate score when a mistake from Villa 'keeper Brad Guzan enabled Nikola Kalinic to head home. If that was bad enough, events took a decidedly worse turn not long after when Kalinic put Rovers two up on the night. Luckily, Villa were able to reply almost immediately when Ashley Young's cross wasn't properly cleared and Stephen Warnock levelled the aggregate scores. Five minutes before half time Blackburn defender Chris Samba was dismissed for a foul on Gabriel Agbonlahor inside the box, and the resultant penalty was smashed home by Milner. If the first half had been exciting, the second was surreal. First Richard Dunne scored after 53 minutes, although it was officially classed as an own goal from Nzonzi, then Agbonlahor put Villa three ahead on aggregate with a strike that really should have been given to Milner. Although the Villa winger wasn't credited with this one, his incisive through ball then saw Emile Heskey race through the Blackburn defence to put Villa 5–2 ahead on the night. This should have put the tie beyond doubt, but after such excitement there was no possibility of it ending quietly. From the re-start Martin Olsson's acrobatic overhead kick gave Blackburn a third goal and with five minutes remaining Brett Emerson's mis-hit shot somehow eluded everyone in a crowded penalty area including Villa 'keeper Guzan, who was seeing his hopes of playing in the final recede as every attack by the visitors seemed to have ended up in the back of his net. Villa still held a two-goal advantage, but anything could have happened before the final whistle. Ashley Young ensured that the drama would continue until the end with an injury time goal that gave Villa an unlikely 6–4 win on the night and led to a good-natured pitch invasion from thousands of supporters celebrating their club's first final for ten years. In truth, it was never a great game, nor a particularly nail-biting one. The outcome was never in any doubt from well before half-time, when Villa scored their second goal and Rovers were reduced to ten men. But it will always be remembered for the number of goals scored and what the result meant. As the announcement on the TV screens as the pitch invaders were making their way back into the stands put it, *"Please leave the stadium and make your way to Wembley."*

— CLARET & BLUE BLOOD —

Villa players who were boyhood fans of the club include:

Peter McParland (340 games, 120 goals)
Gary Shaw (208 games, 78 goals)
Ian Taylor (255 games, 43 goals)
Harry Parkes (345 games, 4 goals)
Mark Walters (200 games, 47 goals)
Tony Daley (241 games, 38 goals)
Zat Knight (26 games, 1 goal)

— GREAT VILLANS: PETER McPARLAND —

Peter McParland: star of the 1957 FA Cup win

Born in Newry, Co Down, in 1934, Peter McParland joined the Villa from Dundalk United. That he made little initial impact can be seen from the fact that his first two league games were 15 months apart. But after this slow start, McParland's rise was meteoric, and he became a Northern Irish international at the age of 20.

The peak of Peter McParland's Villa career was undoubtedly the FA Cup run of 1957. In the first semi-final against West Bromwich Albion he twice scored an equaliser. Then with Albion beaten in a replay, he was the star man in a controversial final.

McParland will always be remembered for his challenge on United keeper Ray Wood, which led to the United player being stretchered off with concussion. Hard he may have been, but McParland played to the letter of the law, and if Wood couldn't get out of the way of McParland's perfectly legal shoulder charge it was certainly not the fault of the Villa winger. McParland later scored the two goals that won the game against a United side reduced to ten men by Wood's departure (no substitutes were permitted in those days).

McParland's other great feat took place during the 1958 World Cup, where all four home nations won through to the final stages and his Northern Ireland side did best of all, reaching the quarter-finals. McParland played the tournament as centre-forward, scoring four goals, and showing that he was equally at home in the centre as on the wing.

Indeed, one of McParland's greatest assets was his versatility. In his early days he was a wing-half, for Villa he played mainly on the wing, Northern Ireland often preferred him at centre-forward and yet his Villa and international colleague Danny Blanchflower regarded Peter as the best British inside-forward of all time.

He played 340 games for the Villa, scoring 120 goals. For a player who spent most of his domestic career as a winger, this is a remarkable record. Considering that the Villa side he played in invariably struggled, it was phenomenal. For many years the opposition needed just one tactic – stop McParland – such was his influence on a club that was in decline almost through his Villa career. He was later to say, "Players turned up at any old time and the way that they trained was a farce – just walking round the track or even going for a smoke."

After many years propping up a team unworthy of his talents, McParland moved to Wolves in January 1962 for £30,000. His stay at Molineux was a short one, and he moved first to Plymouth and then to Worcester City, in the Southern League, before trying his luck in the fledgling North American Soccer League. Here he played for Atlanta Chiefs, who were coached by his former colleague and future Villa manager Vic Crowe. McParland then returned home to become player/manager with Irish League side Glentoran, where his chief scout looked at a youngster named George Best before deciding he was too small to make the grade.

He coached around the world in such unlikely places as Libya (his time there coming to an unscheduled end when Colonel Gadaffi banned football), Hong Kong and Kuwait, before finally retiring to the South Coast. He still attends games at Villa Park, and is a regular at functions organised by the Aston Villa Former Players Association, where even legendary Villa players regard him with awe.

— GREAT VILLANS: PAUL MCGRATH —

Paul McGrath: Aka 'God'

There's no argument, Paul McGrath is the best post-war Villa player. When comparatively young Villa fans say it, that's one thing. When supporters who've been around since the thirties say it, you have to agree.

Born in Ealing, London, in 1959, McGrath's early life as a mixed-race child in a Dublin children's home was often akin to a horror story. He joined the local St Patrick's Athletic side and then transferred to Manchester United, where his heavy drinking and knee problems led to his being advised to retire. He was eventually sold to Villa in the summer of 1989 for £425,000.

McGrath's arrival at Villa Park led to mutterings from some supporters that the club had bought another has-been. Villa manager Graham Taylor realised what a problem he'd acquired when McGrath turned up to sign his new contract the worse for wear, then played in at least one match while under the influence and attempted to kill himself, all within his first few weeks with his new club.

However, Taylor and physio Jim Walker performed a miracle by reviving McGrath's career, and he won the Villa Player of the

Year award as the team finished runners-up in the old First Division in 1989/90. McGrath was to win the award for a phenomenal six consecutive seasons as managers Joszef Venglos, Ron Atkinson, and Brian Little continued to obtain top-class service from a player who continued to defy medical science. He rarely trained, he occasionally went missing, and he was never able to conquer his alcoholism. But Paul McGrath became not only a Villa legend, he was the finest defender in Europe at an age when mere mortals would be thinking about winding down their careers. The nickname 'God' was aptly bestowed by supporters who idolised him.

It's difficult to call one of McGrath's notable achievements the pinnacle of his career. There was the PFA Player of the Year award in 1992/93, the Coca-Cola Cup final the following season, when McGrath defied a crippling shoulder injury to help Villa beat his former club in the final, or one of the countless immaculate performances, particularly during the end of his Villa Park career, when he more than made up for a declining physical ability with peerless reading of the game and sublime anticipation. Maybe Paul McGrath's finest hour came when helping the unfancied Republic of Ireland into the last eight of Italia 90, or four years later, when the 34-year-old defender defied the 90 degree heat of New Jersey and the onslaught of eventual finalists Italy to enable his side to pull off a shock victory.

Eventually, McGrath lost his place in the Villa side and moved to Derby during the early part of the 1996/97 season. In total he played 315 games for Villa, scoring nine goals. 51 of his 83 international caps (eight goals) were won with Villa, making McGrath the club's most-capped player.

— CRUEL AND UNNATURAL PUNISHMENT —

George Cummings was a full-back who captained Villa in the immediate post-war period. He was famous for being the only defender to master the legendary Stanley Matthews and also because he served, as far as we can tell, the longest suspension ever imposed on a Villa player.

Cummings' nickname, the 'Granite Hard Full-Back', gives some indication as to his playing style, yet he was never regarded as a particularly physical player. However, in a war-time friendly on Christmas Day 1942, 9,000 fans watched Villa play at Leicester.

Quite what Cummings did wrong has been lost in the mists of time. No newspaper reports covered the full details of the incident and there are no official records. Yet Cummings was sent off and as a result was suspended the following month *sine die*. He subsequently missed 16 games, including all of that year's War Cup ties.

Cummings' suspension was eventually rescinded in August 1943, in time for the beginning of the new season.

— CHAMPIONS V: 1899/1900 —

The end of the century saw Villa's fourth title win in five years, and their fifth overall. However, despite a playing record that bore comparison with their previous triumphs, the team was beginning to rely on experience and character to grind out results rather than winning by sheer footballing ability.

	P	W	D	L	F	A	Pts
Aston Villa	**34**	**22**	**6**	**6**	**77**	**35**	**50**
Sheffield United	34	18	12	4	63	33	48
Sunderland	34	19	3	12	50	35	41
Wolverhampton Wanderers	34	15	9	10	48	37	39
Newcastle United	34	13	10	11	53	53	36
Derby County	34	14	8	12	45	43	36
Manchester City	34	13	8	13	50	44	34
Nottingham Forest	34	13	8	13	56	55	34
Stoke	34	13	8	13	47	45	34
Liverpool	34	14	5	15	49	45	33
Everton	34	13	7	14	47	49	33
Bury	34	13	6	15	40	44	32
West Bromwich Albion	34	11	8	15	43	51	30
Blackburn Rovers	34	13	4	17	49	61	30
Notts County	34	9	11	14	46	60	29
Preston North End	34	12	4	18	38	48	28
Burnley	34	11	5	18	34	54	27
Glossop	34	4	10	20	31	74	18

— 1966 AND ALL THAT —

Who was the first Englishman to touch the ball at the 1966 World Cup final? It wasn't Bobby Moore, Geoff Hurst or even goalkeeper

Gordon Banks. It was, in fact, future Villa player Neil Rioch, who was a ballboy at the game and handed the ball back into play when it was knocked out by West Germany straight from the kick-off.

— VILLA PARK III: THE NORTH STAND —

The Witton End was originally part of a huge expanse of terracing that ran the full length of Villa Park and held around 40,000 people. Also known as the Barracks end, it was semi-circular to make room for the cycle track that formed a notable part of Villa Park until the beginning of the First World War.

The development of the Witton End took place over an extended period during the 1920s and early 1930s, with the old wooden terraces concreted over and metal crush barriers installed. This part of the ground was then virtually ignored for over forty years, but maintains a strong hold on many supporters' affections. As the Holte End began to attract the more vocal elements of the Villa support, so the Witton was regarded as the area of the ground where fathers would take their children and the growing numbers of away supporters would congregate. Many modern supporters still remember the Witton End as their first Villa Park home.

With no roof and a grass bank behind the terraces, the Witton End became an outdated embarrassment and when Villa's finances became steadier as the team's fortunes improved, plans were put in place for its replacement.

The Witton End was closed for the latter part of 1976/77, and by the start of the following season the £1 million North Stand was ready for business. Such speed was even more remarkable as the stand was the most modern in English football at the time, featuring a goalpost construction in which columns placed outside the supporters' field of view supported the roof, and a double level of executive boxes.

The top tier of the North Stand originally held 4,500, although this was later reduced to make room for corporate areas. The downstairs terrace had room for 5,500. At first this was split between home and away fans, but following outbreaks of violence in 1978, the entire terrace was given over to away supporters.

New offices were added from 1980–82, under the auspices of

a company part-owned by Villa stadium manager Terry Rutter. In mid-1982 an internal report found that invoices totaling over half the cost of the refurbishment could not be accounted for, and the West Midlands Police became interested in the case, although it was later claimed that the final bill for the work was not a great amount more than it should have been. Nevertheless, in 1985 Rutter and his partner Harry Moore were given suspended sentences for defrauding the Football Trust, the judge leaving no doubt that former chairman Ron Bendall would have joined them in the dock had he not died some time earlier. Although the amounts involved may seem trifling now, they left Villa in a parlous financial state, at a time when the European Cup-winning side was in need of rebuilding.

The perimeter fence that had been in place since the construction of the North Stand was removed in 1990, following the Taylor Report, and 2,900 seats installed. What is now known as the North Stand lower was increasingly given over to Villa supporters until away fans were finally located elsewhere for all but occasional cup matches in 2007, meaning that for the first time in almost 30 years, Villa supporters were able to regularly watch their team from behind the Witton End goal.

— SUDDEN DEATH —

Villa's penalty shoot-out results:

Date	Competition	Result	Shoot-out score
Sept 5th 1979	League Cup round two	Colchester 2 Villa 2*	Won 9–8
Feb 3rd 1993	FA Cup round four replay	Wimbledon 0 Villa 0	Lost 6–5
Feb 27th 1994	Coca-Cola Cup semi-final	Villa 4 Tranmere 4*	Won 5–4
Sept 29th 1994	UEFA Cup round one	Villa 1 Inter Milan 1*	Won 4–3
April 2nd 2000	FA Cup semi-final	Villa 0 Bolton 0	Won 4–1

* aggregate score

Villa also lost 5–4 on penalties in a Worthington Cup quarter-final at West Ham on December 15th 1999. However, the game was replayed after West Ham were found to have fielded an ineligible player and Villa subsequently won 3–1.

— WARTIME SERVICE —

The trawler HMT *Aston Villa* was part of a fleet of 'little ships' named after football clubs in the 1930s. She was built in 1937 in Middlesbrough at a cost of £29,352, weighed 546 tonnes and was 173ft long. Ominously for those who believe in omens, she had a slight accident entering Grimsby docks prior to her official launch and caused damage of £3 16 shillings and sixpence to a pier. The new trawler began her maiden voyage on September 7th 1937 and on the outbreak of war two years later was requisitioned by the Admiralty to serve as an anti-submarine vessel. While taking part in the evacuation of Allied troops from Norway in May 1940 the *Aston Villa* came under sustained aerial bombing and was sunk in the Namsen fjord off the Arctic Sea, some 100 miles north of Trondheim, in the early hours of May 2nd. The ship's bell was recovered by divers in 1951 and is displayed in the Namsos Cultural House, close to where she was sunk.

— GREAT VILLANS: GARY SHAW —

Gary Shaw: Midlands superstar

Born in the Birmingham suburb of Kingshurst in January 1961, Gary Shaw was a lifelong Villa supporter who grew up watching Brian Little from the Holte End. He would go on to exceed even his hero's achievements, but sadly, Shaw's career ended in the same tragic way.

There is a story that as a schoolboy Shaw played for non-league Coleshill Town and Villa promised them a £50 fee for his registration – which was never paid. He joined Villa from school, making his debut two months later, and took advantage of Little's injury problems the following season to establish himself in the first team.

The arrival of Peter Withe during the summer of 1980 provided the perfect foil for Shaw, and he contributed 20 goals to the team that won the championship. Withe supplied the muscle and physical presence; Shaw put the ball in the back of the net. His eye for goal drew comparisons with Denis Law, his model good looks made him the David Beckham of his day and a glittering career in every way seemed assured. In the words of Villa photographer Terry Weir, "To have the privilege of watching Gary that season was to watch England's star striker for the next ten years."

Shaw won every Young Player of the Year award there was to win in 1980/81 and his part in Villa's European Cup triumph of the following season saw his star spread ever wider as he was voted UEFA Young Player of the Season. It's no exaggeration to say that in the Midlands at least, Gary Shaw was every bit as much a star as his Brummie contemporaries Duran Duran.

The following season saw Shaw score a personal best of 24 goals, but disaster struck during the first month of the 1983/84 season. Playing in a league game at Nottingham Forest, Shaw went down under what seemed to be an innocuous challenge, but Forest's Ian Bowyer, attempting to pull his opponent to his feet, inadvertently caused a serious knee injury from which the player never fully recovered. At the age of 22, his top-flight career was as good as over. Coming just weeks after his team-mate Gordon Cowans suffered a broken leg that meant he missed an entire season, Shaw's injury was a major factor in the team's decline.

Shaw spent the next five seasons attempting a comeback, and to his credit refused to take the easier option of retirement. After 208 first-team games and 78 goals, he eventually left Villa on a free transfer in the summer of 1988 and played for KB Copenhagen and the Austrian club Klagenfurt. Returning to England, he spent time with Walsall and Shrewsbury Town, for whom he scored what was then the fastest-ever Football League hat-trick in just four minutes and 32 seconds in December 1990, before ending his playing career in Hong Kong. Shaw spent some time working for Villa as a youth team coach and is now employed by the Press Association and in the local media.

— BOADROOM BATTLES: PART TWO —

By the mid-sixties Aston Villa were in decline. The club was relegated to the Second Division for just the third time in their history in 1967, and no-one was under any illusion that there would be a quick return to the top as there had been on the previous two occasions. The Shareholders Association called an Emergency General Meeting in January 1968, and although they were unable to win control, unveiled a shadow board with the aim of toppling the existing directors. Discontent grew until, in November of that year, a meeting was called by supporters at Digbeth Civic Hall, where it was announced that the board had agreed to seek new buyers. Many names were mooted, but eventually a consortium headed by then Birmingham City director Douglas Ellis was to prove successful. Their takeover of the club was a precursor to a period when events in the Villa boardroom were every bit as newsworthy as those on the pitch.

With Ellis in the chair and Tommy Docherty as manager Villa were galvanised, gates trebled and an air of optimism swept the club. Unfortunately, this did not prevent relegation to the Third Division, by which time Docherty had been sacked. The club finally won promotion back to Division Two in 1972, and celebrated with open warfare once more breaking out in the Villa Park boardroom.

The rest of the board had grown tired of Ellis attempting to hog the limelight, and forced a vote of no confidence that led to his resignation and replacement as chairman by fellow-director Jim Hartley. An EGM was the natural outcome and against a backdrop of 'Ellis Villa' or 'Aston Villa,' accusation and counter-accusation was hurled back and forth.

There could only be one winner; Ellis was still enormously popular amongst the rank and file Villa supporters, who loved his charismatic manner and remembered how the club had been run before his arrival. Indeed, many wondered how anyone could find fault with such a man at the end of a successful season. Hartley was forced out of office and with Warwickshire CCC captain Alan Smith and former Villa star Eric Houghton installed as directors, Ellis's position was secured. By now, all pretence that the Villa was run by a board of equals had gone. In less than four years, the new board that had arrived in December

1968 had all, with one exception, left. The club was, indeed, Ellis Villa.

After celebrating one promotion with a boardroom battle, it was almost inevitable that Villa should do the same the next time they went up. They returned to the First Division in May 1975, yet Villa supporters were surprised to learn before the year was out that Doug Ellis had resigned as chairman, claiming that the work he had set out to do in 1968 had now been completed. His replacement was Sir William Dugdale, chairman of Severn Trent Water and a true English country gent. It later transpired that Ellis, far from stepping down willingly, had been the victim of a palace coup with the rest of the board, once more tired of his claims to be Mr Aston Villa, demanding his resignation.

Sir William remained as chairman until the summer of 1978, when he resigned along with fellow-directors Harry Cressman and Alan Smith in protest at the growing power being wielded by Ron Bendall, who had by then become Villa's biggest shareholder. There were reports that Bendall and Ellis had carved the club up between them, but such ideas were shattered during the early part of the 1979/80 season, when Villa Park was the scene of another bitter power struggle (see *Boardroom Battles: Part Three*, page 110).

— YOUNGEST AND OLDEST —

Jimmy Brown holds two records that will almost certainly never be beaten. He made his Villa debut away at Bolton on September 17th 1969, aged 15 years and 349 days, to become the club's youngest-ever first-team player. Then three seasons later, Brown became Villa's youngest captain, at the age of 19.

An FA Youth Cup winner in 1971/72, and winner of the 1972/73 Terrace Trophy for Villa's player of the year, Brown seemed assured of a glittering career. However, for whatever reason, his potential remained unfulfilled and he left Villa Park in the summer of 1975, aged 21, after 85 appearances. He played for a while in the lower divisions, tried his luck abroad, but retired from the game altogether in 1981, aged 28, an age when players should be approaching their peak.

At the other extreme, Peter Schmeichel won virtually every major honour in the game during his time with Manchester

United. He left Old Trafford in 2000 and surprisingly turned up at Villa Park on a free transfer the following summer. Schmeichel's first game for Villa, against Spurs on August 18th 2001 made him, at the age of 37 years and 277 days, Villa's oldest debutant. He then topped this feat by scoring against Everton on October 20th 2001 to become Villa's oldest goalscorer at the age of 37 years, 337 days. This was also the first Premiership goal ever scored by a keeper.

Villa's oldest-ever player was Brad Friedel, who initially gained this distinction against Manchester United in February 2011 and broke his own record with every further appearance, the last of which came against Liverpool on May 22nd 2011, when he was aged 40 years and four days.

— RECORD VILLA PARK ATTENDANCES —

First Division/Premier League: 69,492 v Wolves, December 27th 1949
Second Division: 68,029 v Coventry City, October 30th 1937
Third Division: 48,110 v Bournemouth, February 12th 1972
FA Cup: 76,588 v Derby County, March 2nd 1946
League Cup: 62,500 v Manchester United, December 23rd 1971
European competitions: 49,619 v Barcelona, March 1st 1978

At the other end of the scale, the smallest crowd to attend Villa Park for a competitive first-team fixture is 2,900 for the Division One game against Bradford City on February 13th 1915.

— YOUTHFUL PROMISE —

Villa have won the FA Youth Cup on three occasions. The results in each final were:

1971/72

Villa 1	Liverpool 0
Liverpool 2	Villa 4 (aet)
(Villa won 5–2 on agg)	

1979/80

Manchester City 1	Villa 3
Villa 0	Manchester City 1
(Villa won 3–2 on agg)	

2002/03

Everton 1	Villa 4
Villa 0	Everton 1
(Villa won 4–2 on agg)	

— AWARD-WINNERS —

The *Villa News and Record* has long been regarded as one of the best programmes in the country and has won the Programme of the Year award on seven occasions: in 1971, 1972, 1973, 1977, 1978, 1990, 1992 and 2005.

— CRAZY NIGHT —

Some of the best memories Villa supporters have are from atmospheric European nights. Celta Vigo in the 2000 Intertoto Cup was one of the most memorable, but not for the quality of the football.

For starters the game was played at the Hawthorns, Villa Park being unavailable due to the rebuilding of the Trinity Road stand. Then, when the match got underway, the unheralded Celta forward Bennie McCarthy tore Villa apart, scoring after 11 minutes to put his team 2–0 up on aggregate. However, impressive as McCarthy may have been, he was nowhere near as busy as Swiss referee Dieter Schock, who booked six players in the opening half-hour.

Schock dismissed Celta's Juan Velasco for timewasting – after just 26 minutes – before giving Villa two ludicrous penalties shortly before half-time. Paul Merson missed one, Gareth Barry scored the second. The second half continued in the same farcical manner as the first. Ian Taylor was sent off, seemingly for being fouled, and was followed by Alan Thompson, while a total of 13 yellow cards were shown. Schock's incompetence was summed up by his blowing the final whistle with two minutes remaining and having to call both teams back to resume play when his error was pointed out by an assistant referee. To make matters worse, McCarthy had already scored again to send Villa out of the competition 3–1 on aggregate.

— GREAT VILLANS: ERIC HOUGHTON —

Eric Houghton: a great servant to the Villa

In 1927, a young left-winger from Lincolnshire turned up at Villa Park for a one-day trial. The story goes that he brought with him enough clothes for a fortnight, and if this is true we can only marvel at his foresight because the youngster was Eric Houghton, who went on to serve the club with distinction, both on and off the pitch, over a period which covered eight decades.

Houghton first made his name in the memorable 1930/31 season, when he scored 30 of Villa's record 128 league goals. In total, he made 392 first-team appearances, scoring 170 goals, many of them during that halcyon time in the early 1930s when Villa were twice runners-up in the First Division and played what many regarded as the finest football in the club's history. He also played seven times for England, and would surely have had a longer international career had not war intervened.

Houghton possessed a fearsome shot in either foot, once scoring a free-kick from fully 40 yards, and was reckoned to have missed just seven out of 79 penalties he took during his Villa career.

After the war, Houghton left Villa Park to first play for and then manage Notts County, whom he led to the Third Division (North) title during his first season in charge. He was also a talented cricketer, who captained the Warwickshire 2nd XI for several years.

In 1953, Houghton returned to Villa Park as team manager in succession to George Martin, setting into place the youth policy that would bear fruit several years later under the managership of Joe Mercer. Houghton's time in charge saw undistinguished league performances, but in his defence the team was beginning the slide that was to lead to near-disaster during the following decade. For the first time since league football had begun, Villa's top players were wanting to leave and adequate replacements could not be attracted. However, Houghton's reign will be forever remembered as the time in which Villa won the FA Cup for the seventh time, beating Manchester United 2–1 in the final of 1957.

Houghton resigned as manager two years later. The reasons for his departure were shrouded in mystery, but it was later thought that he felt let down over bonuses he felt he was entitled to receive following the cup win, as well as being worn out by the arguments which were raging behind the scenes, as the board yet again attempted to interfere in the manager's duties.

That was virtually the end of Houghton's managerial career. He spent some time at Rugby Town, of the Southern League, before returning to work for the Villa Supporters' Association as a full-time organiser. Houghton served as a director under Doug Ellis's chairmanship, resigning after the boardroom battles of 1979. He was later to become the club's only permanent vice-president and was regarded as the elder statesman of Aston Villa. A warm and immensely popular figure, Houghton's death in 1995 marked the end of an era. He was the symbol of a time in which the club were held in high regard around the world both for the brilliance of their achievements and for the values they upheld. No-one upheld them better than Eric Houghton.

— GREAT GAMES 5: THE SHOULDER OF GOD —

Aston Villa 2	**Manchester United 1**
McParland (2)	Taylor

May 4th 1957: FA Cup Final
Wembley
Att: 100,000

Manchester United's Busby Babes were at their peak in 1956/57. They'd won the league by eight points, scoring more than 100 goals in the process, and only Villa could prevent them from winning the double as the FA Cup final kicked off.

The game's major talking point, one still remembered half a century later, took place in the sixth minute, when Villa winger Peter McParland shoulder-charged Ray Wood, the United keeper, leaving Wood badly concussed and unable to continue. Looking at film of the incident it's hard to claim that the collision was an accident, but McParland acted perfectly within the laws of the game and their interpretation at the time.

With no substitutes permitted, United had to rearrange their defence, with wing-half Jackie Blanchflower going in goal. The Reds' ten men coped with Villa's attacks until half-time, but, as the second half wore on, the notoriously tiring Wembley turf sapped at their strength and gave Villa extra impetus. Duncan Edwards had been forced to move to the unfamiliar role of centre-half and neither he nor the 19-year-old Bobby Charlton could make any impact against the Villa half-back line of Crowther, Dugdale and Saward.

Wood had returned from hospital to take his place as a virtual passenger on the wing in a game Villa were now dominating. After 67 minutes Villa captain Johnny Dixon sent over a centre from which McParland hit a fierce header that would have beaten any goalkeeper in the country, let alone a makeshift replacement. Five minutes later, Dixon again provided for McParland, this time his shot hitting the bar and the Irishman's follow-up volley giving the Villa a two-goal lead.

United threw everything into an attempt to retrieve the game, and with six minutes left pulled one back, after which Wood returned to goal for a furious finale in which the league champions desperately, but unsuccessfully, battled for an equaliser.

The final whistle sounded to herald Villa's seventh FA Cup triumph. While the sympathy of the neutrals was with United, there was not a Villa supporter in the ground who would have disagreed with the claim that theirs had been the better team on the day and that, ten-man opposition or not, Villa's victory had been well-deserved.

— WE ARE (STILL) THE CHAMPIONS —

In the last decade of the 19th century Villa weren't just the best football team in the land, they were also the one and only English professional baseball champions. 1890 saw the formation of a league which comprised four teams, although Derby were to drop out before the end of the season. Villa won the league, with a side that featured several ex-footballers, plus James Cowan and John Devey of the team that later won the double. The league folded after its inaugural season and there has never been a national professional baseball league in Britain since then. Villa can therefore claim to still be the reigning league champions, a title they have held for over 120 years.

— FROZEN STIFF —

A modern-day record of sorts was established during the 1978/79 season when Villa drew 2–2 at home on Boxing Day, then due to bad weather they didn't play at home again until 67 days later, beating Birmingham City 1–0 on March 3rd 1979. In that time the team played three away games, drawing two and being knocked out of the FA Cup by Nottingham Forest.

— LOYALTY BONUS —

On July 24th 1998 Villa signed David Unsworth from West Ham for £3 million. On July 29th the player asked for a transfer and two days later agreed to join Everton, for the amount Villa had paid for him just a week earlier. Unsworth didn't get two signing-on fees, nor was he awarded a testimonial.

Villa manager John Gregory stated that Unsworth wanted to leave Villa because he hadn't realised how far Villa Park was from his home and that his wife didn't like him being away for so long. Humorous though this explanation was, it later emerged that Unsworth had signed for Villa without knowing of the interest from his former club Everton, who would have been his preferred choice, and the story about travelling times was thought up to prevent embarrassment all round – except for the player, who for years endured chants about his domineering wife whenever he appeared at Villa Park.

— MR ASTON VILLA —

In the number of column inches gained, even Ron Atkinson has to take second place to one man . . .

"Women and horses work for nothing."
Doug Ellis, explaining why he became Villa's first paid director

"When he was recovering in hospital, one of our sons said the words 'Doug Ellis.' The heart monitor went shooting up and all the nurses came rushing in."
Rosina Barton, widow of former Villa manager Tony, on her husband's recovery from a heart attack

"It was a total surprise. I was gobsmacked."
On the news that the new Witton Lane stand was to be named after him as a 70th birthday present

"They're calling it 'The Other Doug Ellis Stand'."
Chelsea chairman Ken Bates on news that Villa were building a new Trinity Road structure

"I will never sack another manager."

And he never did, although the next three all resigned

"I have never had a controlling interest in Aston Villa and I have no wish to do so."

During the 1979 boardroom battles

"If I was after a player I'd ask Doug what he thought. Sooner or later I'd manipulate him to mention the player I wanted, then I'd chip in and say 'good shout' and I'd get the player because Doug would say he'd recommended him – provided he came good.".

Graham Taylor, possibly the only Villa manager to get the better of Ellis

"We had a love-hate relationship. Well, he loved me."

Taylor a few years later

"My trouble is that I'm a devil for seeing the other fellow's point of view."

Ellis, on his biggest weakness

"The trouble is that the chairman thinks we're like Manchester United but acts small. He's stuck in a time warp."

Villa manager John Gregory

"This is my life. I sign every cheque and kick every ball. They'll carry me out of here in a box."

On his love for Villa

"I'm a would-be professional who in the end wasn't good enough."

Looking back at his playing career

"It has been my sincere pleasure to have been involved with Aston Villa these many years, both as chairman and as a substantial shareholder. The club has been an enormous and immensely enjoyable part of my life."

After selling out to Randy Lerner, August 2006

"Doug Ellis's 35 years at Villa straddle the game's dizzying transformation through the boom of the 1990s. He is a monument to the ways in which many football directors of his generation were able, ultimately, to make fortunes for themselves."

Journalist Dave Conn, writing in the *Guardian*

— THE BEST FRIENDLY EVER —

Whatever any other club might think, the greatest friendly of all time took place on February 21st 1972, when 54,437 paid then club record receipts of £35,000 to see Third Division Villa take on Santos, captained by Pele. Part of Villa's plans to offset the disappointment felt by not attaining promotion the previous season, the club staged a series of friendlies against high-profile foreign opposition in order to keep the Villa name in the public imagination. They had already played Polish champions Gornik Zabrze the previous December, with a respectable crowd of 14,662 attending a match that ended 1–1.

The build-up to the Santos game was shrouded in doubt as an energy crisis caused by striking miners had led to intermittent power cuts. To counteract this threat, Villa brought in three generators to ensure the fixture would go ahead.

The game was played in a lively spirit, but initially with only one of the Holte End floodlights working. This caused problems at the start of the second half, when the Holte End lights began working properly, but one of the Witton End lights then dimmed. Santos protested that this had been a deliberate ploy to ensure they were defending in near-darkness for both halves, and Pele threatened to lead his team-mates off the field. Eventually, World Cup referee Jack Taylor persuaded the Brazilians to resume play, only for the lights to dim later on in the game when light and heating were switched on in the dressing rooms.

Villa eventually won 2–1, with goals by Pat McMahon and Ray Graydon while Edu replied for Santos. McMahon also emerged with the star prize of Pele's shirt. But the result was immaterial. Another great night had entered Villa Park folklore.

Villa had also lined up a friendly against German side Bayern Munich, which was played in January 1973. The game ended 1–1 but, despite the presence of Sepp Maier, Franz Beckenbauer and

Gerd Muller in the Bayern side, attracted a crowd of just 23,000 and the idea of staging more high-profile games in the future was dropped.

— THE GREAT MYSTERIES —

Two questions which have been asked almost since the club's formation are; where did the name Aston Villa come from, and why do Villa play in claret and blue? The first of these is easily answered. Aston Villa was the name of a Georgian country house built on Lozells Road. Although the house demolished in the 1830s, well before the football club was formed, the area became known as Aston Villa. Some twenty years later the Aston Villa Wesleyan Chapel was built, and from here came the cricket club from which the Villa evolved. Coincidentally, there was another Aston Villa Cottage on Heathfield Road, where the famous 1874 discussion under the lamppost took place. The origin of the club's colours is less well-known and has been the subject of much debate over the years. Many theories have been put forward, most of which can easily be debunked. For example, the belief that the colours were taken from the favourite Scottish clubs of William McGregor and his wife, Rangers and Hearts, is discounted because McGregor had no interest in football until moving to Birmingham and the clubs in question were comparatively unknown at this time. Equally unlikely is the theory that claret and blue were the colour of the decorations inside the nearby Barton's Arms, which was not built until 1901. Villa historian and former programme editor Bernard Gallagher claimed to have found minutes of a meeting at which Villa player of the 1880s, Ollie Whateley, a graphic designer by trade, was commissioned to design a kit for the first team. As Villa began wearing claret and blue regularly in 1887 and Whateley had been forced to give up playing the previous year, it may have been that he was awarded the commission as a gesture of sympathy. Noted football historian Simon Inglis, however, has expounded a simpler theory. This was the great period of high Victorian architecture, with many buildings incorporating elaborate interior design. One notable feature of such buildings was inevitably Minton tiles, whose most popular pattern was claret (or chocolate) and blue. There were many such buildings in the Aston and Handsworth areas, which at the time made up Villa's heartlands, and the club may simply have copied this colour scheme.

— UNSUNG HERO —

Many people have worked tirelessly behind the scenes at Villa Park, but the most recognisable in living memory was Terry Weir, club photographer for over 20 years. Born in Aston, Terry became famous for sitting behind the goal Villa were attacking at almost every game, home, away or during the Villa's many European adventures. Whatever the weather, Terry snapped the action and his eye for the unusual meant that he was responsible for capturing many of the more quirky moments in Villa's recent history. He even climbed to the top of a nearby tower block before one evening kick-off for a shot of Villa Park's unique floodlights shaped in the form of an 'A' and a 'V'.

Terry retired as club photographer following a motoring accident in 1994, but remained a regular visitor to Villa Park, where his jovial manner (he was a great fan of Laurel and Hardy) and wealth of anecdotes made him a firm favourite amongst anyone who met him. A collection of his photographs, *The Weir and The Wonderful*, was published in 2002 and quickly became the fastest-selling book in the club's history. Terry died in February 2004, and news of his death saw mourning on a scale usually reserved for great players.

— THE HARDEST FOOTBALLER EVER —

Frank Barson was born in Grimesthorpe, Yorkshire, in 1891. Apprenticed to a blacksmith, he was booked in his first competitive game and became known as a centre-half not to be trifled with. Barson came to prominence playing for Barnsley, where he served a two-month suspension after being sent off in a friendly against Birmingham, and on one occasion had to be smuggled out of Goodison Park to avoid an angry mob following an FA Cup tie with Everton.

George Ramsay and Frederick Rinder, the Villa directors responsible for scouting and signing new players, were convinced that Barson would improve the team and a deal was struck. He maintained a business in Sheffield and refused to move to Birmingham despite Villa's repeated insistence that he should do so. This cost him dearly once, when he and goalkeeper Sam Hardy, who like Barson lived in Chesterfield, were forced to walk seven miles to Old Trafford in pouring rain after missing a rail connection. Naturally, Barson was the best player on the pitch that afternoon.

Barson's living arrangements caused further controversy on the opening day of the 1920/21 season, when he and Clem Stephenson missed a defeat at Bolton due to further problems on the railways. Both were suspended by the Villa board for 14 days but Barson still refused to move. He was appointed team captain for the rest of the season, although it's not known whether this was the board's decision or whether Barson decided he wanted the job and nobody dared argue with him.

Probably the most famous story about Frank Barson concerned the 1920 FA Cup final, when he was warned about his behaviour by referee Jack Howcroft — in the dressing room before the match started. Barson had one of the few quiet games of his career, but was still instrumental in Villa's 1–0 victory over Huddersfield Town.

For Barson, a lengthy career at any single club would have been impossible. Following a match against Liverpool, he invited a friend to wait in the dressing room while he got changed and this drew a rebuke from a director. The disciplinarian Rinder became involved in the argument and when Barson refused to apologise, his Villa days were numbered. Even Frank Barson couldn't get the better of Fredrick Rinder.

Villa offered him terms to re-sign at the beginning of the following season, but Barson refused to play for the team again, joining Manchester United in late August 1922. Barson was regarded as a hero in Manchester, although he didn't welcome undue flattery. He was so sick of such attention that on the opening night of his pub he gave the business to his head waiter.

Barson once received a good luck telegram prior to a game – from a pair of criminals in the condemned cell – and there is a story that towards the end of his career, he didn't feel he was getting the pay rise he deserved, so helped contract negotiations along by meeting his manager carrying a gun.

After leaving Old Trafford, Barton wound down his career at Watford, Hartlepools United, Wigan and finally Rhyl Athletic, where, with some kind of symmetry, he celebrated his last game, at the age of 40, by being sent off once more.

— THE BUS PASS CHAIRMAN —

Quite what Norman Smith would have made of the billionaire tycoon Randy Lerner flying the Atlantic in his own private jet to visit Villa Park is unknown. Smith, who was Villa chairman in the period before Doug Ellis took office in 1968, was said to have never owned a house nor learned to drive. After retiring from his job in the education department of the old Birmingham City Corporation, Smith would catch the bus every day from the suburb of Handsworth, where he lived in lodgings, to his office at Villa Park.

In contrast, Sir William Dugdale must be one of the most aristocratic men to have graced a football club's boardroom. Sir William, whose namesake and ancestor was one of the foremost historians and archivists of the 17th century, served as Villa chairman from 1975 until his resignation from the board three years later. A direct descendant of William the Conqueror, he is the second Baronet Dugdale. Sir William served as a captain during World War II, winning the Military Cross. Amongst other notable achievements he took part in a round-the-world air race during which he was forced to make a rapid landing after almost running out of fuel, and rode in the Grand National. The uncle of Conservative Party leader David Cameron, Sir William is still a Villa Park regular in his eighties.

— GREAT VILLANS: JOHNNY DIXON —

The last Villa player to lift the FA Cup

Johnny Dixon was born in Spennymoor, County Durham, in 1923. He came to the Villa's attention after writing to the club asking for a trial, and so impressed the club's coaching staff that he signed at the end of the Second World War, easing his way into the inside-forward spot he held for many years.

Like his long-time colleague Peter McParland, it was Dixon's misfortune to play for the Villa at a time when the club was at a low ebb. There was an air of despondency around the place and successive managers were unable to bring about the success supporters felt they deserved as of right. Like the board, many of the Villa Park crowd could still recall the days when Villa were the greatest team in the world and they believed that anything less than the best was not good enough. As club captain, Dixon often came in for harsh treatment, although he accepted this as part of the job description. "It hurt, but they were entitled to their opinion," he said many years later of the crowd's reaction.

Yet there was one shining success during Dixon's time, and he played a leading role in this memorable achievement. He will always be remembered as captain of the 1957 FA Cup-winning team. Photographs of him receiving the cup abound around Villa Park, yet Dixon has always said that he would be delighted to lose the dubious distinction of being Villa's last cup-winning captain.

Dixon played 430 games for the Villa and scored 144 goals, a highly-creditable total considering he spent much of his career in a struggling side, and during his latter years he became a wing-half. Relegation in 1959 and the emergence of the Mercer Minors saw Dixon lose his place in the first team and he played just five league games during his last two seasons. His final game for the Villa was the last match of the 1960/61 season, when he scored the fourth goal in a 4–1 victory at home to Sheffield Wednesday. Making his first-team debut that day was a Scottish left-back named Charlie Aitken, who would go on to enjoy an even longer Villa career. Dixon was appointed youth team and then reserve team coach, eventually losing his job in 1967 as the club slumped to the Second Division and manager Dick Taylor was sacked along with the rest of his backroom team.

Dixon bore no malice towards his only professional club, and continued to turn out for the Villa Old Stars until well into his 70s. He then became president of the Aston Villa Former Players' Association and was a regular visitor to Villa Park until shortly before his death in January 2009.

— PROPHET WITHOUT HONOUR —

Villa's influence on football is well known, but one Villa man who played a major role in the game's worldwide development remains better known abroad than at home. Jimmy Hogan made his name coaching in Central Europe either side of the First World War, working alongside the legendary Hugo Meisel to make Austria the pre-eminent national side on the continent during this period. However, Hogan was an unpopular figure in British football due to his working for the Hungarian side MTK whilst interned during the war. The FA Secretary at the time, Frederick Wall, called him a traitor and most people thought the game here had nothing to learn from what was happening overseas. With the situation on the Continent growing ever-more perilous, Hogan returned to Britain in the summer of 1936 and became Villa manager following relegation to Division Two. He led the club to promotion two years later and was building a top-class team when war once more interrupted his career and the club temporarily closed down as a full-time entity in 1939. Hogan returned to Villa Park some years later as youth team coach, laying the foundations for what would become known as the Mercer Minors despite then being in his seventies. The Hungarian side that beat England at Wembley in 1953 paid tribute to him; Sandor Barcs, then-president of the Hungarian Football Federation said, "Jimmy Hogan taught us everything we know about football." In later years Hogan did finally receive the credit his innovative ideas deserved. His successor as Villa manager Joszef Venglos, another man who could claim to have been ahead of his time in English football, said of Hogan, "He was a great influence on European football," while Sir Matt Busby called him, "A great man in every way."

— FINAL COUNTDOWN 2 —

Villa have appeared in seven League Cup finals, winning five:

August 22nd 1961, Millmoor (1st leg)
Rotherham United 2 **Aston Villa 0**
Webster 51
Kirkman 55

Rotherham: Ironside, Perry, Morgan, Lambert, Madden, Waterhouse, Webster, Weston, Houghton, Kirkman, Bambridge

Villa: Sims, Lynn, Lee, Crowe, Dugdale, Deakin, McEwan, Thomson, Brown, Wylie, McParland
Att: 12,226

September 5th 1961, Villa Park (2nd leg)
Aston Villa 3 **Rotherham United 0** (aet)
O'Neill 67
Burrows 69
McParland 109

Villa: Sidebottom, Neal, Lee, Crowe, Dugdale, Deakin, McEwan, O'Neill, McParland, Thomson, Burrows

Rotherham: Ironside, Perry, Morgan, Lambert, Madden, Waterhouse, Webster, Weston, Houghton, Kirkman, Bambridge
Att: 30,765

May 23rd 1963, St Andrews (1st leg)
Birmingham City 3 **Aston Villa 1**
Leek 14, 52, Thomson 45
Bloomfield 66

Birmingham: Schofield, Lynn, Green, Hennessey, Smith, Beard, Hellawell, Bloomfield, Harris, Leek, Auld

Villa: Sims, Fraser, Aitken, Crowe, Sleeuwenhoek, Lee, Baker, Graham, Thomson, Wylie, Burrows
Att: 31,580

May 27th 1963, Villa Park (2nd leg)
Aston Villa 0 **Birmingham City 0**

Villa: Sims, Fraser, Aitken, Crowe, Chatterley, Lee, Baker, Graham, Thomson, Wylie, Burrows

Birmingham: Schofield, Lynn, Green, Hennessey, Smith,

Beard, Hellawell, Bloomfield, Harris, Leek, Auld
Att: 37,921

February 27th 1971, Wembley
Aston Villa 0 **Tottenham Hotspur 2**
Chivers 78, 82

Villa: Dunn, Bradley, Aitken, Godfrey, Turnbull, Tiler, McMahon, Rioch, Lochhead, Hamilton, Anderson

Spurs: Jennings, Kinnear, Knowles, Mullery, Collins, Beale, Gilzean, Perryman, Chivers, Peters, Neighbour
Att: 100,000

March 1st 1975, Wembley
Aston Villa 1 **Norwich City 0**
Graydon 79

Villa: Cumbes, Robson, Aitken, Ross, McDonald, Robson, Graydon, Little, Leonard, Hamilton, Carrodus

Norwich: Keelan, Machin, Sullivan, Morris, Forbes, Stringer, Miller, MacDougall, Boyer, Suggett, Powell
Att: 95,946

March 12th 1977, Wembley
Aston Villa 0 **Everton 0** (aet)

Villa: Burridge, Gidman, Robson, Phillips, Nicholl, Mortimer, Deehan, Little, Gray, Cropley, Carrodus

Everton: Lawson, Darracott, Jones, Lyons, McNaught, King, Hamilton, Dobson, Latchford, McKenzie, Goodlass
Att: 100,000

March 16th 1977, Hillsborough (replay)
Aston Villa 1 **Everton 1** (aet)
Kenyon og 79 Latchford 89

Villa: Burridge, Gidman, Robson, Phillips, Nicholl, Mortimer, Deehan, Little, Gray, Cowans, Carrodus

Everton: Lawson, Bernard, Darracott, Lyons, McNaught, King, Hamilton (Pearson), Kenyon, Latchford, McKenzie, Goodlass
Att: 54,840

April 13th 1977, Old Trafford (second replay)

Aston Villa 3	**Everton 2**
Nicholl 80	Latchford 38
Little 81, 118	Lyons 82

Villa: Burridge, Gidman (Smith), Robson, Phillips, Nicholl, Mortimer, Graydon, Little, Deehan, Cropley, Cowans

Everton: Lawson, Robinson, Darracott, Lyons, McNaught, King, Hamilton, Dobson, Latchford, Pearson, Goodlass
Att: 54,749

March 27th 1994, Wembley

Aston Villa 3	**Manchester United 1**
Atkinson 25	Hughes 83
Saunders 73, 89	

Villa: Bosnich, Barrett, Staunton (Cox), Teale, McGrath, Richardson, Fenton, Townsend, Saunders, Atkinson, Daley

Man Utd: Sealey, Parker, Irwin, Pallister, Bruce (Sharpe), Kanchelskis, Ince, Keane, Giggs (McClair), Cantona, Hughes
Att: 77,231

March 24th 1996, Wembley

Aston Villa 3	**Leeds United 0**
Milosevic 20	
Taylor 55	
Yorke 88	

Villa: Bosnich, Charles, Wright, Ehiogu, McGrath, Southgate, Townsend, Draper, Taylor, Milosevic, Yorke

Leeds: Lukic, Kelly, Radebe (Brolin), Palmer, Weatherall, Pemberton, Gray, Ford (Deane), Yeboah, McAllister, Speed
Att: 77, 065

February 28th 2010, Wembley

Aston Villa 1	**Manchester United 2**
Milner 5 (pen)	Owen 12
	Rooney 74

Villa: Friedel, Cuellar, Collins, Dunne, Warnock; A Young, Milner, Petrov, Downing; Agbonlahor, Heskey.

Manchester United: Kuszczak; Rafael, Vidic, Evans, Evra; Valencia, Fletcher, Carrick, Park; Owen, Berbatov.
Att: 88,596

— BOARDROOM BATTLES: PART THREE —

By the early part of the 1979/80 season, Doug Ellis had become increasingly frustrated at his peripheral role in the boardroom, with Harry Kartz in the chair and Ron Bendall the power behind the throne. Seizing on the excuse that Ron Saunders had acted rashly in allowing several star players, including Andy Gray and England international John Gidman, to be sold, Ellis called yet another EGM.

The ensuing battles were played out in front of the national media, and were seen as a struggle between Ellis and Ron Saunders. Neither man made any secret of his dislike of the other, with Saunders regarding Ellis's criticisms of the club's transfer polices as a slur on his own managerial ability.

After weeks of bitter argument, during which time Ellis was regularly criticised for putting his ambitions above those of the club, the battle lines were finally drawn for the EGM and subsequent AGM, which would take place on the Villa Park pitch on successive nights. Two acrimonious evenings followed, described by witnesses as having brought greater shame on the club than any act of hooliganism ever had.

The mood of the initial EGM was overwhelmingly pro-Ellis. As ever he won the support of the small shareholders, although the Shareholders' Association, a group with influence far exceeding its size, came out against him with a half-page advertisement in the *Birmingham Post*. Bendall had the backing of the supporters on the Holte End, more out of loyalty to Saunders than anything else, as well as his own personal holding. A show of hands resulted in an overwhelming victory for the Ellis faction, which included Eric Houghton. A card vote was called, and no-one could be certain of its outcome.

What eventually won the day for Bendall was the support of the former directors who had fallen out with Ellis over the years and now wished to exact their revenge. With the exception of Houghton, every man who had ever served on the board with Doug Ellis voted against him. Ellis lost his vote of no confidence, and was also defeated in his attempts to get Kartz, Bendall and Bendall's son Donald removed as directors.

Ellis resigned from the Villa board, later selling his shareholding to Bendall, but was probably working out ways of returning even as he drove out of the car park. His return came quicker than expected, and after a period of success that would have surprised even the most fervent Villa supporter.

In December 1982 news broke that Ron Bendall was to sell his shareholding in Aston Villa to former player and director Harry Parkes. Yet just as the sale was due to be completed, a further announcement was made to the effect that the new chairman of Aston Villa was to be none other than Doug Ellis. Quite why Bendall went back on his agreement with Parkes and sold to Ellis has never been explained, but with over 40 per cent of the club's shares under his control, Doug Ellis was never again seriously challenged.

Protest movements grew up, and although the club's AGM once more became the source of much acrimony, with the revived Shareholders Association calling votes of no confidence and making token attempts to add their leaders to the board, Ellis's block vote, even after Villa floated on the Stock Exchange in 1997, was enough to quell any rebellion.

The acquisition of the club by Randy Lerner in the summer of 2006 and his subsequent purchase of the company's entire share capital means that the days of boardroom in-fighting are over, at least for the foreseeable future.

— GREAT VILLANS: RON ATKINSON —

Big Ron!

Ron Atkinson first joined Villa as an amateur in the fifties, spending much of his time with the 'A' team, in the Birmingham Works League. A wing-half with more enthusiasm than talent, Atkinson played for Headington United during their march from the Southern League to Division Two, changing their name to Oxford United in the process, and after an apprenticeship in non-league management, joined Cambridge United in1974. United won the Fourth Division title three years later and Atkinson was approached to manage West Bromwich Albion, where he assembled an attractive side.

In 1981 he moved on to Manchester United, where he won the FA Cup twice before being sacked after a poor start to the 1986/87 season. He took over at the Hawthorns once more, then had a brief 96-day stay with Atletico Madrid before joining Sheffield Wednesday. An unlucky relegation in 1990, was followed by an immediate return to the First Division, with the Rumbelows Cup won as a bonus.

Atkinson had been linked with the Villa job every time the vacancy arose, and the call finally came in strange circumstances. In May 1991 he originally accepted the job, changed his mind and agreed to stay at Hillsborough and then completed a full-circle turnaround when becoming Villa manager.

Under Atkinson, Villa played football that at times verged on the sublime. In the inaugural Premiership season, 1992/93, Villa looked likely champions for much of the campaign but ran out of steam and finished eventual runners-up to a Manchester United side who hit peak form at the right time.

The following season saw Atkinson gain a modicum of revenge when Villa met United in the Coca-Cola Cup final. A tactical masterstroke led to Atkinson playing a 4-5-1 formation with youngster Graham Fenton the surprise package of a 3–1 victory. However, Ron came under fire when the team hit a bad run of form at the beginning of the 1994/95 season, accused of being more concerned with furthering his media career than with managing the club. A 4–3 defeat away at Wimbledon led to his dismissal, and although supporters reacted with fury at the news, eight wins in his last 34 games was justification enough for Doug Ellis. Ironically, Atkinson remains the last Villa manager to have been sacked, every departure since having either been by virtue of resignation or 'mutual consent.'

Atkinson then joined Coventry City, working in tandem with Gordon Strachan as the Sky Blues established themselves as a mid-table Premiership side. He returned to Sheffield Wednesday, helping them avoid relegation, and his final high-profile managerial position was with Nottingham Forest, in debt and doomed at the bottom of the Premiership. Atkinson was unable to keep them up and retired from the game in 1999 to work full-time in the media.

Ron became the lovable eccentric of football, his curious phrases leading to the term 'Ronglish' entering the vocabulary. However, some unwise remarks about Chelsea's Marcel Desailly in 2004 led to his departure from ITV and a brief ostracising from the media.

In 2007 Atkinson was briefly appointed director of football

at Kettering Town and then Halesowen Town, also working on cable TV and for Radio WM. He remains one of the most colourful characters in football, and there are few who have a bad word to say about him. He certainly retained his popularity at Villa Park, and with good cause. When Ron Atkinson was around, the club was guaranteed to be in the news.

— A TRAGIC TALE —

Of all the men who have played for the Villa, surely none had as tragic a tale as Arthur Sabin. Born in the Villa stronghold of Kingstanding, Sabin signed as a professional in January 1957, on his 18th birthday. He made his league debut three months later in a 5–0 win at home to Sheffield Wednesday, becoming the Villa's youngest-ever goalkeeper.

Great things were expected of Sabin, who played one further league match, a 1–1 draw at home to Spurs that November. Tragically, the player was taken ill during a reserve game the following month and was rushed to hospital suffering from what was believed to be heart failure. He died on March 5th 1958, less than two months after his 19th birthday.

— SECOND FIDDLE IN THE SECOND CITY —

Bragging rights have never been so firmly established as they were during the 2007/08 season. This period of second city supremacy saw Villa beat Blues in the Premier League 2–1 at St Andrews and 5–1 at Villa Park. Villa reserves beat their Blues counterparts 2–0 at home and 1–0 away, while the youth team won 4–1 and 3–0 in their respective matches.

— GREAT GAMES 6: VILLA ARE BACK —

Aston Villa 2	**Manchester United 1**
Lochhead	Kidd
McMahon	

December 23rd 1970: League Cup semi-final, second leg
Villa Park
Att: 62,500

Anyone who was in the crowd for the 1970/71 League Cup semi-final second leg with Manchester United will agree – it was more than just a football match, it was a turning point in the club's history. Decades of neglect had culminated in the previous season's relegation to the Third Division, but here was a sign that the club was on their way back.

The first leg at Old Trafford had resulted in a surprising 1–1 draw and United, European champions just three seasons earlier, were determined to put matters right. This was the Manchester United of George Best, Bobby Charlton and Denis Law, and even if they might have been a bit past their peak, they were still surely more than a match for a side from the third tier.

When Brian Kidd opened the scoring after 14 minutes it appeared that the natural order would be restored, but from that moment on Villa were in control. Spurred on by a backing that was likened in one match report to that which Brazil enjoyed in the 1970 World Cup final, Villa got over their early setback and deservedly equalised in the 37th minute when Brian Godfrey's cross eluded everyone except Andy Lochhead, who slammed the ball into the back of the Holte End net.

From then one there would only ever be one winner. As the noise from the Villa Park crowd grew from intense to frenzied, United's team seemed to grow old in a matter of minutes. Only George Best and goalkeeper Jimmy Rimmer (who would himself take part in many future great Villa Park occasions) prevented a humiliation, but neither could stop Villa from taking the lead after 72 minutes, when another cross from Godfrey was knocked into the box by Willie Anderson, and Pat McMahon headed home.

The noise grew ever louder, Villa's play grew likewise in confidence and although they scored no more goals, they never looked like conceding an equaliser. The final whistle saw scenes of joy that many had believed would never be witnessed at Villa Park again. As Dennis Shaw said in his *Evening Mail* report the following day, "Never has Villa Park been so electrified with emotion. Never have Villa so deserved a golden prize. Never can a set of supporters have played such a prominent part in a team's display."

The game had repercussions that went on long after the last supporter had gone home and the Villa Park floodlights had been extinguished. Villa went on to lose 2–0 to Spurs in the final at Wembley but this was of secondary importance. The club had regained its pride and the belief amongst everyone, from Doug Ellis down, was that nothing was now impossible.

— GREAT VILLANS: ALLAN EVANS —

Ron Saunders acquired players from the most unlikely sources, and the unlikeliest of the lot must surely have been picking up a central defender from the forward line of Scottish first division side Dunfermline Athetic. Originally signed as a centre-forward for £20,000 in the summer of 1977, Allan showed his goalscoring prowess by scoring six goals in a reserve game, and made his first appearance at Villa Park in the UEFA Cup tie with Barcelona in Match 1978. His robust approach enabled Villa to score two late goals in the tie but Saunders soon decided that his best position would be further back, helping form a perfect partnership with fellow Scot Ken McNaught as the title-winning team began to take shape. Allan was still proving to be a handful in the opposition penalty area, scoring nine goals in 1979/80, although his somewhat robust attitude to defending produced an equal number of yellow cards and two dismissals. This disciplinary record saw Evans miss the opening of the memorable 1980/81 but once available he was a first-choice in the side until the end of the season. Allan played in 39 of the 42 league games, scoring seven goals including a memorable winner against Blues at St Andrews and the second against Middlesbrough in the final home game of the season. Evans made just four appearances for Scotland, scandalously overlooking Villa players not being the exclusive preserve of England managers, and took part in the 1982 World Cup finals in Spain. By this time he had won a European Cup winner's medal, and added the following year's Super Cup to his list of honours. McNaught's departure in 1983 broke up their partnership and Evans never achieved the same level of consistency with others as he had enjoyed during the glory years. But he remained as committed to the Villa cause as ever, turning down the opportunity to move in favour of helping what proved a doomed struggle against relegation in 1987. By now team captain, Evans enjoyed a renaissance to his Villa career with the arrival of Graham Taylor as manager and helped Villa win promotion in 1988. Allan left the club in 1989, the last of the title winners to depart (discounting Gordon Cowans' returns) and the club's sixth-highest appearance-maker. He finished his playing career with Leicester City then moved abroad for a while before linking up with Brian Little at Darlington, for whom he made one final league appearance, Leicester and the duo's return to Villa Park in 1994. After further time working with Little at Stoke and Albion, Allan returned to Scotland to manage Morton, before quitting the full-time game and moving to Cornwall, where he has held several coaching and managerial positions.

— MONEY, MONEY, MONEY —

What's the most valuable goal ever scored by a Villa player? The obvious answer is Peter Withe's winner in the European Cup final of 1982. However, in direct cash terms Stewart Downing's goal against Liverpool at Villa Park on the final day of the 2010/11 season was worth far more. Downing's was the only goal of the game, and such was the crowded nature of the final league table that the extra two points it earned took Villa from 14th to ninth place and earned them an extra £3,783,780 in prize money.

— YOU'LL NEVER BEAT THE VILLA! —

Clubs Villa have never lost to in league games are:

Brentford (Played 6, Won 5, Drawn 1)
Darwen (Played 4, Won 3, Drawn 1)
Gillingham (Played 2, Won 1, Drawn 1)
Lincoln City (Played 2, Drawn 2)
Scunthorpe United (Played 2, Won 2)
Stockport County (Played 2, Won 2)
Tranmere Rovers (Played 4, Won 3, Drawn 1)
York City (Played 4, Won 3, Drawn 1)

Apart from Lincoln, the only teams who Villa have never beaten are:

Mansfield Town (Played 4, Drawn 1, Lost 3)
Northampton Town (Played 2, Lost 2)
Walsall (Played 4, Drawn 3, Lost 1).

— CHAMPIONS VI: 1909/10 —

Villa's sixth title was won on the back of impressive home form. They were unbeaten in 17 out of 19 games at Villa Park and finished five points clear of runners-up Liverpool. Supporters who had grown impatient for another title were doubtless certain that further success would not be long in coming . . . little could they have known it would be 71 years before the trophy returned to Villa Park.

	P	W	D	L	F	A	Pts
Aston Villa	**38**	**23**	**7**	**8**	**84**	**42**	**53**
Liverpool	38	21	6	11	78	57	48
Blackburn Rovers	38	18	9	11	73	55	45
Newcastle United	38	19	7	12	70	56	45
Manchester United	38	19	7	12	69	61	45
Sheffield United	38	16	10	12	62	41	42
Bradford City	38	17	8	13	64	47	42
Sunderland	38	18	5	15	66	51	41
Notts County	38	15	10	13	67	59	40
Everton	38	16	8	14	51	56	40
Sheffield Wednesday	38	15	9	14	60	63	39
Preston North End	38	15	5	18	52	58	35
Bury	38	12	9	17	62	66	33
Nottingham Forest	38	11	11	16	54	72	33
Tottenham Hotspur	38	11	10	17	53	69	32
Bristol City	38	12	8	18	45	60	32
Middlesbrough	38	11	9	18	56	73	31
Woolwich Arsenal	38	11	9	18	37	67	31
Chelsea	38	11	7	20	47	70	29
Bolton Wanderers	38	9	6	23	44	71	24

— FINAL COUNTDOWN 3 —

European glory!

Villa have appeared in one European final, famously winning the European Cup in 1982:

May 26th 1982, de Kuip, Rotterdam
Villa 1 **Bayern Munich 0**
Withe 67

Villa: Rimmer (Spink), Swain, Williams, Evans, McNaught, Mortimer, Bremner, Shaw, Withe, Cowans, Morley

Bayern: Muller, Dremmler, Horsmann, Weiner, Augenthaler, Kraus (Niedermayer), Durnberger, Brietner, Hoeness, Mathy (Guttler), Rummenigge
Att: 39,776

— GREAT VILLANS: BILLY WALKER —

Generally regarded as the finest Villa player between the wars, Billy Walker was born in Wednesbury, in 1897. He first had trials with Villa at the age of 16, signing as an amateur in 1915, then turning professional in January 1920. He went straight into the first team and won an FA Cup winners medal just four months later, then a runners-up medal in 1924, both finals being played against Newcastle United. Yet Walker's finest moments were to come some time later, with the arrival of centre-forward Pongo Waring and the emergence of Walker's partner on the left wing, Eric Houghton.

Possessed of mercurial talent and what would then be described as matinee idol looks, Walker was the darling of the Villa Park crowd in a way that would not be emulated until Gary Shaw emerged almost 60 years later. With ball control and passing ability to rival his uncanny eye for goal, Walker was the perfect inside-forward, ideally complementing Waring's robust manner and the skills of Houghton.

He went on to play 531 games for the Villa, a figure only exceeded by the remarkable Charlie Aitken, and scored 244 goals, a club record. Walker also played 18 times for England, scoring eight times. He was a first-team regular for 14 seasons, and scored double figures in 12 of them.

In November 1934 Walker retired from playing, at the age of 36, in order to take the job of Sheffield Wednesday manager. Under Walker's managership Wednesday won the FA Cup in 1935, but were relegated two seasons later and Walker resigned his position in November of that year, his replacement being Notts County boss Jimmy McMullan, who in 1934 had been appointed Villa's first-ever manager.

After a time at non-league Chelmsford City, Walker took the job of managing Nottingham Forest in 1939, and remained at the City Ground for 21 years. During this time the club were relegated to the Third Division (South), yet their committee retained faith in Walker and he steered the club back to Division One, as well as winning the FA Cup in 1959, before being forced by ill-health to retire from football the following year. Billy Walker died in 1964, at the age of 67.

— GREAT GAMES 7: 'DEVASTATION. PURE AND SIMPLE' —

Aston Villa 5	**Liverpool 1**
Gray (2)	Kennedy
Deehan (2)	
Little	

December 15th 1976: Division One
Villa Park
Att: 42,841

Forty-five minutes of perfection. That's the only way to describe Villa's first half performance in the 5–1 rout of Liverpool on December 15th 1976.

Supporters who have only begun following football during the Premiership era may be amazed to learn that such a game could take place without TV cameras being present, but that's what happened. Despite Liverpool being champions and on their way to achieving a league title and European Cup double, playing at the home of the team who were the First Division's most entertaining side, the one camera crew which each ITV region was allowed to use that night was elsewhere. Derby County were unveiling their new record signing Derek Hales and Gary Newbon, ATV's then head of sport, chose to cover events at the Baseball Ground. Therefore the only record of what's reckoned to be the best football played by a Villa team since the war is a few photos from newspaper archives and the memories of the 42,841 spectators. What they saw was:

9 minutes: John Robson crossed to Andy Gray, who rose from ten yards out to beat Liverpool goalkeeper Ray Clemence to the ball and head into an empty net.

12 minutes: Dennis Mortimer burst forward into the Liverpool half with the type of run that would become his trademark, feeding John Deehan, who ran on to slide the ball under Clemence from the edge of the area.

20 minutes: Gray's pass was deflected into the path of Deehan, who shot low from an acute angle ten yards out to beat Clemence at the near post.

31 minutes: John Gidman received the ball inside his own half and moved down the wing before pushing a short ball to Brian Little, who cut inside and hit a brilliant 15-yard shot that curled into the top corner for the best goal of the night.

40 minutes: A half-cleared Liverpool centre fell to Ray Kennedy, whose shot through a crowd of players beat the unsighted Villa keeper Jake Findlay.

44 minutes: Mortimer's near-post corner was met by Gray, who beat Phil Thompson to the ball and headed home from five yards with Clemence beaten once more.

The half-time whistle signalled a thunderous ovation from the stunned crowd, while the second half was, quite naturally, an anti-climax. It was Liverpool's heaviest defeat since 1963, and one that hasn't been beaten since then. No wonder the *Daily Mirror's* report of the match the following morning was headed, 'Villa for England'. Meanwhile, *The Liverpool Echo*'s headline described their team's defeat as 'Devastation. Pure and Simple.'

— FROM THE TERRACES —

The first Villa fanzine was the short-lived *Witton Wisdom*, which began in February 1989 and ran to six issues. This was followed by *Heroes and Villains*, which began in August 1989 and is still going strong.

Other independent publications at Villa Park have included *Never Loved Ellis*, *Missing Sid* (which became the *Villa Bugle*), *Off the Junction*, the *Witton Wag*, *Holy Trinity* and the most obscure of the lot, *Ellis Out*, a handwritten effort which lasted for just one issue.

— IN RESERVE —

Since the Premier Reserve League was set up in 1999–2000, Villa have been one of its most successful clubs, having won a joint-record four regional titles (Northern in 2003/04, Southern in 2007/08, 2008/09 and 2009/10) and the play-off final in 2009. Before then they had won the Central League three times, in 1928/29, 1963/64 and 1992/93.

— GREAT VILLANS: ANDY GRAY —

Andy Gray: a rare talent

Born on St Andrew's Day 1955, Gray made his name in the Scottish Premier League. With Dundee United before Ron Saunders broke Villa's then-transfer record by paying £110,000 to bring the player to Villa Park in October 1975.

Gray's first appearance in claret and blue is still regarded as one of the finest Villa debuts, as he scored his team's only goal in a 2–1 defeat to Manchester United in the League Cup. Gray's all-action style soon made him a favourite with supporters, who loved his bravery, commitment and reluctance to back down from any challenge, whether it came from opponents or referees.

The following season saw Gray cement his place in Villa Park folklore with 25 goals as Villa ended 1976/77 fourth in the league, their highest position for over 40 years, and won the League Cup. Gray's magnificent contribution made him the first player to win both the PFA Player and Young Player of the Year awards in a single season. These achievements, though, began Gray's rift with Ron Saunders, who refused to allow the player to attend the awards dinner as it took place three days before the League Cup final replay. With his taste for glamorous girlfriends, fast cars and an ability to hit the news headlines as well as the sports pages, Andy Gray was the first true celebrity to emerge from Midlands football. He even owned a nightclub, the Holy City Zoo in Birmingham city centre.

However, like many talented Villa players before and since, Gray failed to enjoy a long and successful career with the club. He missed out on selection for the Scottish World Cup squad in1978, and the rest of his Villa Park career was raked with injury and controversy.

Gray asked for a transfer at the beginning of the 1979/80 season claiming he "wanted to win things", although it was generally reckoned that the real reason for his departure was yet another fall-out with Saunders. He eventually signed for Wolves for what was, briefly, a world record fee of £1.47 million. He scored the winning goal for his new club in the 1980 League Cup final and later won the league championship and Cup Winners Cup with Everton before returning to Villa Park in the summer of 1985 for £150,000.

Gray's two seasons in his second spell at Villa are best forgotten. Injuries had begun to take their toll on the player, while the team and club were in decline. Relegation and the arrival of Graham Taylor led to Gray's departure to Albion, for £25,000, and his career ended with a spell at Rangers, the team he supported as a boy. Here, title success meant that Andy Gray became one of the few players to win both Scottish and English league championship medals. His time at Villa had seen him score 78 goals in 205 games.

On his retirement from football, Gray began a career as a TV pundit, most notably for Sky. He returned to Villa Park for a third spell, as assistant to manager Ron Atkinson for the 1991/92 season, but when asked to choose between his two jobs, preferred full-time TV to the strains of management.

Gray divides opinions like few other Villa players. His supporters consider him one of the greatest Villa forwards of all time. His detractors would say this contribution was overshadowed by the manner of his departures and his often outspoken opinions of former managers. All, though, would agree that when he was on form Andy Gray was a rare talent.

— PITCH INVADERS —

Villa Park played host to two strange characters during the 1950s. They soon became part of the matchday furniture and left as quickly as they arrived, although in one case his behaviour would be remembered for many years to come.

This was the supporter known by the descriptive nickname of 'The Man Who Walks On His Hands.' He would slip quietly out of the crowd at the old Witton Bank before the match and make his way onto the pitch, where to loud cheers he would perform a handstand on the halfway line and walk on his hands to the Holte End, flicking his cap in front of him. Whatever the condition of the pitch he would always arrive at his destination, flip back onto his feet, kick his cap into the goal and dash onto the Holte End terrace. Here he would take up a collection then melt into the crowd, anonymous once more.

The police would always attempt to apprehend him, but they would invariably get to the Holte End just as The Man Who . . . vanished. A cynic might suggest that they enjoyed the show as much as everyone else did and had no wish to see it ended. Eventually the object of their half-hearted interest was identified as the appropriately named Lenny Hands, an itinerant newspaper seller from Hockley. These days he would almost certainly have been arrested and banned from the ground.

Another Villa Park character of the period was Darkie, the club's self-styled mascot. Darkie was a black man (or a white man blacked up – no-one knew which) who dressed in a top hat and tails and stood at the mouth of the players' tunnel before the game, shaking hands with the Villa team as they ran out onto the pitch. Again, such a figure would be unthinkable at a modern ground, but back then no-one took much notice. In fact, so little attention did 'Darkie' attract that most supporters fail to remember him at all.

Both men disappeared from the matchday scene without comment. Maybe they, like so many other supporters of the era, grew tired with Villa's steady decline and decided to spend their Saturday afternoons elsewhere.

— GREAT VILLANS: GERRY HITCHENS —

Born almost on the doorstep of Villa Park in Rawnsley, Staffordshire, in 1934, and later living in Kidderminster, Gerry Hitchens should have been snapped up by the Villa when he left school. However, the club's scouting system was obviously faulty and it took until Hitchens was 23 before a £22,500 fee brought the player from Cardiff City in December 1957.

Hitchens was still completing his National Service, as a military policeman in the army at the time, so Villa had to wait until the end of the following season before seeing the best of him in action. By this time Villa had been relegated to the Second Division, and Hitchens set about the lower level's defences with a vengeance. He scored 25 goals in 1959/60, including five in Villa's 11–1 thrashing of Charlton Athletic, the club's biggest-ever victory at Villa Park.

The blond-haired Hitchens' goalscoring ability drew comparison with Pongo Waring, but Hitchens was a more all-round player than his great predecessor in the number nine shirt. Villa returned to Division One as champions, and the following season saw Gerry score 42 goals for the club. He also attracted the attention of the England selectors, being the first Villa player to be picked for England since Tommy Thompson in 1951. Scoring with his first kick of the game on his debut against Mexico, Hitchens inevitably became the target of clubs with greater resources than the Villa.

Despite assurances from chairman Chris Buckley that their star centre-forward was not for sale, Villa supporters knew that he would soon be on his way and so it proved, with Hitchens departing in the summer of 1961 to Italian club Internazionale for a fee of £85,000 and a personal signing-on fee of £12,000, plus a luxury flat and car. He had been with Villa for just four seasons and had scored 96 goals in 160 games.

Hitchens spent nine years in Italy, also playing for Torino, Atalanta and Cagliari. He took part in the 1962 World Cup finals held in Chile, and his international career lasted a total of seven games, in which he scored five goals.

Upon his return from Italy, Hitchens played for Worcester City in the Southern League before retiring. Tragically, Gerry collapsed from a heart attack while playing in a charity game in North Wales in 1983 and died instantly, at the age of 48. His relatively short Villa career and the club's lack of success during this time means that Gerry Hitchens is often overlooked when great players are discussed, but anyone who saw him play, or a brief look at his goalscoring record, will provide ample evidence that he was one of the claret and blue best.

— TOP TEN —

In July 2011 Villa's official website listed what they considered to be the club's top 50 post-war players. Some of the names were rather controversial, but the top ten was as follows:

1. Gordon Cowans
2. Dennis Mortimer
3. Johnny Dixon
4. Paul McGrath
5. Trevor Ford
6. Peter McParland
7. Peter Withe
8. Allan Evans
9. Nigel Spink
10. Charlie Aitken

— VILLA HERE, THERE AND EVERYWHERE —

References to Aston Villa in popular culture include:

- In the BBC comedy series *Porridge*, the character Lennie Godber played by Richard Beckinsale was a Villa supporter.
- Jim Hacker, the eponymous hero of another BBC comedy series *Yes, Prime Minister*, referred to watching both the Villa and his local team, 'Aston Wanderers'.
- The main character in author Joe Gallivan's novel *Oi Ref* is a Villa-supporting referee. Several real-life Villa supporters are mentioned in the book.
- In a further BBC comedy, *Dad's Army*, Private Pike often wore a claret and blue scarf. He never mentioned football but as actor Ian Lavender, who played Pike, was born in the Villa stronghold of Erdington, the significance was clear.
- Villa games have been used as the backdrop for several TV dramas, most notably BBC police series *Juliet Bravo* (Blackburn Rovers v Villa, 1980) and *The Firm* (Crystal

Palace v Villa, 1988). The BBC series *Back-Up* also featured an episode dealing with violence at a football match, in which the supporters were clearly shown as Villa and Liverpool.

- Bob Marley's *One Love/People Get Ready* video shows several Villa players from the 1980/81 season celebrating a goal.
- Arnold Bennett's novel *The Card* has a scene in which the board of the local football club, Bursley, are discussing Villa's recent transfer policy.
- Phillip Larkin's poem *MCMXIV* begins:

Those long uneven lines
Standing as patiently
As if they were stretched outside
The Oval or Villa Park

- In Harold Pinter's play *The Dumb Waiter*, two characters discuss Villa matches they've seen.

— VILLAS WORLDWIDE —

Villa Park is also the name of, amongst other things, a city in California, a village near Chicago, a holiday complex on the Caribbean island of Aruba, a suburb of Denver, Colorado, a ski resort in Bulgaria, and hotels in Bratislava, Warsaw, Venice and New Jersey.

— ASSORTED LEAGUE RECORDS —

Consecutive wins: 9, 1910/11 (plus 11 in the Football League South in 1945/46)
Consecutive defeats: 11, 1962/63
Consecutive games unbeaten: 15, 1909/10
Consecutive games without a win: 12, 1972/73 and 1986/87
Most points in a season (calculated as three for a win): 102, 1971/72

Fewest points in a season (calculated as three points for a win): – 36, 1986/87 (42 game season). Also, the equivalent of 25 points in the 22-game 1890/91 season.
Most goals scored: 128, 1930/31
Fewest goals scored: 37, 1968/69
Most goals conceded: 110, 1935/36
Fewest goals conceded: 32, 1971/72 and 1974/75

— FURTHER READING —

Footballer autobiographies can sometimes not be particularly exciting, but some of the better, if sometimes more harrowing, ones in recent years have been from ex-Villa players. They include:

Hero and Villain – A Year in the Life of Paul Merson (**Willow, 1999**). The author wrestles with the demons of addiction against the backdrop of a roller-coaster season at Vila Park.

Full Time – The Secret Life of Tony Cascarino (**Scribner, 2002**). One of the books which broke the mould of anodyne footballing life stories, this one showed the oft-derided Cascarino as a complex and human character.

Stan: Tackling My Demons – Stan Collymore (**Willow, 2004**). A no-holds barred look at one of football's most controversial characters and the illness which has blighted his life.

Back from the Brink – Paul McGrath (Arrow 2007). The often distressing story of how a traumatic childhood led to an adult life on the edge, made even more dramatic by the writer being one of the finest footballers in the world. One of the blackest football books ever written.

The Real Bobby Dazzler – the Bobby Thomson Story (**DB Publishing, 2010**). Gangsters, rock stars, footballers and assorted sixties celebrities are covered in this story of the George Best of Birmingham – talent, drinking, and all.

Budgie – John Burridge (**John Blake, 2011**). The story of a goalkeeping eccentric who had 29 clubs and played until he was 47, then like many others found that hanging up his gloves was where the problems started.

— RECORD TRANSFERS —

Some of the milestone fees paid by the Villa include:

Fee	Year	Player	Signed from
£250	1895	Jimmy Crabtree	Burnley
£1,000	1913	Andy Ducat	Woolwich Arsenal
£10,500	1934	Jimmy Allen	Portsmouth
£55,000	1968	Mike Ferguson	Blackburn Rovers
£100,000	1969	Bruce Rioch	Luton Town
£200,000	1977	Ken McNaught	Everton
£300,000	1979	David Geddis	Ipswich Town
£500,000	1980	Peter Withe	Newcastle United
£1.5 million	1990	Tony Cascarino	Millwall
£2.3 million	1992	Dean Saunders	Liverpool
£3.5 million	1995	Savo Milosevic	Partizan Belgrade
£4 million	1996	Sasa Curcic	Bolton Wanderers
£7 million	1997	Stan Collymore	Liverpool
£9.5 million	2001	Juan Pablo Angel	River Plate
£9.65 million	2007	Ashley Young	Watford
£12 million	2009	Stewart Downing	Middlesbrough
£18 million	2011	Darren Bent	Sunderland

— GREAT VILLANS: DAVID PLATT —

David Platt: Villa and England hero

Born in Chadderton in 1966, David Platt originally signed for Manchester United as a YTS player during Ron Atkinson's time as manager at Old Trafford. He moved to Crewe Alexandra on a free transfer where he flourished under the managership of Dario Gradi.

Platt moved to Villa, then in the Second Division, for £200,000 in 1988. Although Graham Taylor had reservations about the size of the fee, Platt began to repay his new manager almost immediately, with five goals in 11 matches as Villa gained promotion at the first attempt. The following season saw Platt operating in midfield, scoring regularly as Villa battled to avoid relegation. Then came 1989/90, probably the best season of his career.

Platt's immaculate performances helped Villa finish runners-up in the league and himself to win the PFA Player of the Year award. His great asset was his non-stop running and ability to arrive unseen in the opposition penalty area at the same time as another perfectly flighted ball from team-mate Gordon Cowans.

He also gained a place in the England squad for the World Cup in Italy. Here, Platt came into his own following injury to captain Bryan Robson. His injury-time goal against Belgium was followed by another in the quarter-final victory over Cameroon.

He returned home as one of the heroes of a team that had helped change the public perception of football. No longer was the sport seen as the exclusive preserve of the bellicose hooligan; for good or ill, it was about to become fashionable.

Platt's club performances were one of the few highspots of a disappointing 1990/91 season for the Villa. Towards the end of the campaign it became clear that he saw his future elsewhere and eventually moved to Italian side Bari for what was then a world record fee of £5.5 million. By now Platt was an England regular, and frequently captained the side until losing his place following Euro 96, after winning 62 caps and scoring 27 international goals.

Platt was at Bari for a year, then moved to Juventus, with whom he won a UEFA Cup winners medal, and Sampdoria. He then moved back to England, spending three seasons with Arsenal before retiring from playing in 1998.

Then followed a controversial short spell back with Sampdoria, where he was officially described as 'supervisor in charge' as he lacked the qualifications to coach in Serie A. Platt later managed Nottingham Forest and coached the England Under-21 side. Surprisingly for such an articulate and intelligent footballer, Platt's managerial career has never been a great success. He left Forest after spending heavily and failing to win promotion back to the Premiership, and resigned from the England set-up after his charges missed out on qualification for the 2004 European Championships. He is now a coach at Manchester City.

Platt made a total of 145 appearances for the Villa, scoring 68 goals. However, his place in Villa Park folklore isn't merely confined to what he did on the pitch. His Italia 90 exploits helped transform the national game while his eventual transfer fee helped finance many of Ron Atkinson's subsequent dealings. David Platt was, arguably, the most influential Villa player of the past 20 years.

— ON THE CONTINENT —

Not counting the Intertoto Cup, Villa have played competitive matches in 18 European countries: Austria, Belgium, Croatia, the former Czechoslovakia, the former East Germany, France, Iceland, Italy, the Netherlands, Norway, Poland, Romania, Slovakia, Spain, Sweden, Turkey and the former USSR. Their most common destination has been Spain (six times), followed by Turkey and Italy with three visits each.

— GREAT VILLANS: HOWARD SPENCER —

It could be argued that history has not served Howard Spencer well. When great Villa players of the past are discussed, the man known as the 'Prince of Full-Backs' scarcely rates a mention alongside contemporaries such as Charlie Athersmith and those who came later. Yet Spencer remains the most-decorated Villa player of all time, winning five championships and three FA Cup winners' medals, as well as six England caps.

A product of Albert Road School in Aston, Spencer began his career with Birchfield Trinity before joining the Villa in 1894 and was first-choice in the right-back position for a decade afterwards.

Spencer was the finest defensive thinker of his age, and contributed many an article to newspapers and books in which he stated his belief that football should, above all, be played fairly. In the 1905 *Book of Football* he wrote, "There is nothing to be gained by unfair play. I have always believed that it is possible to get the best results by straight-forward, honest and honorable football."

Not for nothing was Spencer also know as 'Gentle Howard.' It was this honesty that limited his international career to just six appearances, as the England selectors often favoured a more robust approach to the game. But Spencer never needed to make a reckless tackle, as his anticipation inevitably meant that he was in the right place at the right time, ready to intercept an opposition pass and, more often than not, play out of defence rather than utilise the accepted tactic of hoofing the ball in the general direction of his forward line.

By 1904 it was thought that Spencer was past his best and the board dropped him to the reserves. Yet rather than accept the inevitable, Howard fought back, regained his place and even captained the team that won the FA Cup at the end of that season.

Two years later, Spencer left the Villa after making almost 300 first-team appearances, returning to the club in 1909 as a director, a position in which he served for 27 years. It was during this time that he travelled to Tranmere on a scouting mission, recommending that the Villa sign a young forward named Pongo Waring. In 1936, with Villa relegated for the first time, the shareholders sought blood and Spencer, wishing as ever to put the interests of the club above his own personal ambitions, agreed to retire from the board in order to allow the return of Frederick Rinder.

Howard Spencer, by now a rich man following the success of his business, Spencer Abbot Fuel Merchants, died at his home at Four Oaks in 1940. He had served the Villa for almost half a century, during which time they had scaled heights attained by no club before and by very few since. Moreover, he had done so without ever wavering from his belief that honesty and fair play were the most abiding virtues in football. No man was ever a greater credit to Aston Villa.

— UPS AND DOWNS —

Dean Saunders was a popular member of Villa's team under Ron Atkinson, as much for his non-stop effort as for his goalscoring ability. 'Deano,' as he was dubbed by supporters, had a lengthy career at the top level, so it's hardly surprising that he achieved the notable feat of playing at four clubs who have previously won the European Cup – Villa, Liverpool, Benfica and Nottingham Forest. However, what Deano might not be so proud of is his record of having been involved in eight unsuccessful relegation campaigns.

— AERIAL DRAMA —

Villa Park has seen many dramatic moments. Not all of these have come in big games, but they remain in the memory of anyone who witnessed them long after ostensibly bigger occasions have been forgotten. Arguably the most vivid of all these occurred on December 13th 1998, when title-chasing Villa were at home to Arsenal in a game switched to Sunday for live TV.

Villa were two down at half-time when a display by an RAF parachute team ended in near-tragedy. Conditions were poor, with a strong wind gusting, and one of the paratroopers, Flight-Sergeant Nigel Rogoff, was blown into the Trinity Road stand, crashed into the roof and, to the horror of everyone witnessing the event, plummeted 70 feet to the ground.

Paramedics rushed to the scene and the second half was delayed for 20 minutes as they battled to save the stricken man, who, to add to the surreal horror of the incident, was dressed in a Father Christmas outfit. That this all took place in full view of a packed Villa Park crowd as well as millions watching on television further increased the drama of the afternoon

Many people thought the match should have been abandoned, and several distressed spectators left the ground, but when the second half finally got underway Villa's fortunes were transformed. Stan Collymore was at his inconsistent best as Villa ran out 3–2 winners, although the game was of secondary importance and it was only when news broke that Fight-Sergeant Rogoff would survive his ordeal could supporters begin to celebrate a momentous and memorable victory. Seldom has any English football ground witnessed such a dramatic afternoon.

Ironically, this was the third time within a few weeks in which Arsenal had been unwitting witnesses to tragedy. A steward had been killed by their team coach at Coventry while a Champions League game in Greece had seen a Panathinaikos supporter fall to his death from a roof.

Despite later having a leg amputated, Rogoff made an otherwise-full recovery and indeed, married one of the nurses who had looked after him as he recuperated. He attended a game at Villa Park as a guest of the club and was introduced to the crowd at half-time, receiving a hero's welcome. He later unsuccessfully sued the Ministry of Defence for negligence and was later reported to be gathering evidence for a further legal challenge.

— VILLA PARK IV: THE HOLTE END —

Oval in design to allow for the cycle track which ran around the pitch up until 1914, after which both ends were redeveloped to give the ground its now-familiar rectangular shape, generations of Villa supporters grew up paying a few coppers to cheer on their team from the uncovered, often cramped and open-to-the-elements terraces of Villa Park.

There was no particular reason why supporters preferred to stand at one end or the other. More often than not, their choice of terrace position depended on where their bus or tram stopped, and they would often swap ends at half time by walking through either the Trinity Road or Witton Lane enclosures. There was no segregation and no fences to prevent supporters from walking around the ground.

The Holte End, which has been alternatively known over the years as the Church, City and Holte Hotel Ends, was first rebuilt as the outbreak of the First World War put paid to Fredrick Rinder's plans to turn Villa Park into a ground holding 130,000 spectators.

In 1939, the Holte End was further extended, with a nominal capacity of 40,000 in a ground that was reckoned to hold double that. The work was finished by April 1940, and was the only example of football ground redevelopment to take place during the Second World War. The rear half of the Holte was then roofed in 1962 at a cost of £40,000, this work being funded by the club's Supporters Association which was thriving despite the team's lack of success.

By now the Holte End held around 30,000, which made it, along with the Liverpool Kop and the South Bank at Molinuex, one of the largest end terraces in the country. Although it became home to Villa's more vociferous and exuberant support, the Holte tended to be free of the large-scale violence which became commonplace from the late sixties onwards. There were scarcely a handful of occasions when hooliganism went beyond more than a brief scuffle.

Minor refurbishments took place during this period, such as the re-concreting of the terrace steps in the late seventies and the erection of a perimeter fence, as well as a further fence running the length of the terrace, dividing the Holte into two separate blocks, in 1977.

The Taylor Report of 1990 recommended, amongst other things, the abolition of terracing at top grounds by the end of the 1993/1994 season. By now the capacity of the Holte End had been reduced to 19,210, which was still the largest terrace in the country, and the club were faced with the dilemma of how to maintain the ground's capacity. It was first thought that seats would be added to the original terrace and, to help facilitate this, the roof was extended to the front of the terrace. However, it was realised by early 1994 that this arrangement would give unsatisfactory sightlines and that it would be far better to demolish the stand completely and build a new two-tier construction in its place.

The Holte End closed for business in May 1994. Seven months later the Holte Stand was completed. With 5,751 seats upstairs and 7,750 on the lower tier it became the largest single end stand in Britain, built at a cost of £5.6 million, of which £600,000 was donated by the Football Trust. In January 2012 Villa chief executive Paul Faulkner announced that, following discussions with supporters, the club would be interested in examining the possibility of introducing safe standing in a part of the stand, raising hopes that once more Villa fans could stand on the Holte.

— GREAT VILLANS: IAN TAYLOR —

There have been more skilful Villa players than Ian Taylor. Many have enjoyed longer and more successful careers at Villa Park. But none gave more to the club, and few have enjoyed such a relationship with the supporters. The main reason why he is revered even now is that Ian was a Villa fan himself, living the dream of every youngster who ever took their place in the Holte End that they, too, might one day be playing on that Villa Park pitch. Not only that, but he also performed in the same way a fan would, covering every blade of grass, chasing every lost cause, going into every tackle as though his life depended upon winning the ball. Throughout the inconsistent performances of the Little and Gregory eras, the one certainty was that no one could ever accuse Ian Taylor of lacking effort. He began his playing career with Moor Green in the Southern League, moved to Port Vale then Sheffield Wednesday and was eventually bought for £1 million by Brian Little in December

1994. Taylor's first fairytale moment came on his home debut when he scored against Chelsea in front of the Holte End – naturally this was the first game for which the new stand was fully opened. During the following season Ian became a regular in Little's three-man midfield, his box-to-box running a perfect complement to the generalship of Andy Townsend and ball playing of Mark Draper. That season's League Cup final gave another fairytale moment – two years earlier Ian had been amongst the Villa supporters who witnessed the win over Manchester United. Now he was in the side that beat Leeds, scoring the second goal in a one-sided 3–0 win. Taylor spent several more years as a regular in the team, until slipping out of the first team picture during Graham Taylor's return and leaving in the summer of 2003 on a free transfer for Derby, where he was made captain and was the team's top scorer in 2003/04. He then moved to Northampton Town and, after he announced his retirement in 2007, many Villa supporters watched his final match at Sixfields. After hanging up his boots Ian's iconic status amongst the fans was reinforced when he was spotted travelling to several away grounds and sitting with the Villa supporters. He is now a club ambassador and works in the media.

— BY ROYAL APPOINTMENT —

Royalty has made several visits to Villa Park. On January 24th 1924 the Duke of York, later to become King George VI, officially opened the Trinity Road stand, staying on to watch Villa beat Bolton Wanderers 1–0.

On June 9th 1951 Princess (later Queen) Elizabeth watched an exhibition of physical education at the ground as part of a royal visit to Birmingham.

The new Trinity Road stand was opened by Prince Charles on November 12th 2001. In attendance was Jack Watts, 83-year-old Villa Park tour guide, who at the age of six had been present at the opening of the original stand.

Despite being a Villa fan, Prince William has never been spotted at Villa Park. He did, however, attend the club's FA Cup semi-final with Bolton at Wembley on April 8th 2000.

— GREAT VILLANS: DWIGHT YORKE —

'It's up to you Dwight Yorke, Dwiiighht Yooooorke!'

Dwight Yorke's career took a long time to take off, but he briefly lit up the Villa Park stage before leaving in controversial circumstances.

Born in Tobago in 1971, Yorke came to the Villa's attention during the cub's mid-season tour of the island in 1988 (Doug Ellis, naturally, claims that it was he who first noticed Yorke's ability). The initial £10,000 paid to his club, Signal Hill, represents one of the most astute signings any football club has ever made.

Yorke made an uncertain start to his career in England, with former Villa boss Tommy Docherty famously saying, "If he makes it, I'm Mao Tse-Tung". He first came to prominence in the 1991/92 season, when scoring 17 goals in 35 first-team games. Yorke was then surprisingly left out of the side for much of the following two years, being played on the wing or in midfield on the rare occasions he was given a game. Brian Little's arrival as manager led to Yorke being given an automatic first-choice spot up front and he responded with 61 goals in three seasons, including two in the Coca-Cola Cup semi-final with Arsenal and another in the 3–0 win over Leeds in the final. His strike partnership with the unjustly-maligned Savo Milosevic hinted at greater things to come as Little's side showed glimpses of becoming a genuine Premiership force.

But this prowess also attracted the attention of bigger clubs and it was no surprise when Yorke finally moved to Manchester United for a club record fee of £12.6 million in August 1998. By this time, John Gregory was Villa manager and his reaction to Yorke's transfer was the second most famous quote connected with the player: "If I'd had a gun I would have shot him."

Gregory's comments may have helped fuel the anger that many Villa supporters felt towards Yorke. However, calmer heads pointed to the fact that Yorke had been offered an opportunity few players would have declined, and for a while it appeared as though the transfer had been the best for all concerned. Yorke became a hit at Old Trafford, helping his new club win an unprecedented Premiership, FA Cup and Champions League treble in his first season. John Gregory, for his part, invested the windfall provided by this transfer wisely, as Villa led the title race for much of the season before eventually fading away to finish seventh.

Yorke spent four seasons at Old Trafford, but increasingly found himself making more headlines for his lifestyle than his football abilities and moved to Blackburn Rovers, then spent time at Birmingham City. A move to Australian side Sydney FC was short-lived, and from 2006 until his retirement from playing in 2009 Yorke played for Sunderland, with the tabloid headlines behind him. He is now a commentator on Sky Sports.

Dwight Yorke played 247 games for Villa, scoring 97 goals. While his departure may have been better handled, there was no doubt that during his brief, meteoric spell as an out-and-out striker, he was one of the best Villa have fielded.

— THE VILLA PARK TRAGEDY —

Villa Park has always been one of the safest grounds in the country. However, standards were far more lax in the old days and tragedy struck at an FA Cup tie with Arsenal on February 20th 1926. Over 71,000 crammed into Villa Park with an estimated 20,000 locked out, and before kick-off the enormous crowd broke over the barriers and onto the pitch. The worst crushing occurred near the players' tunnel on Trinity Road and one man, Alexander Bartholomew, was taken to hospital in a critical condition, dying the following week.

Villa claimed that the tragedy was not their fault and that there had been room for several thousand more spectators in the ground, despite the gates having been locked well before the crowd began to spill onto the pitch. It was stated at the inquest into Bartholomew's death that 130 stewards and 163 police officers had been on duty at the game and the club could have done nothing more to prevent the fatality. The coroner agreed, returning a verdict of accidental death. And so football failed to heed another warning.

— FOOTBALL VIOLENCE —

Villa supporters have never had a bad reputation, but there were occasions in the supposedly peaceful days of yore when problems occurred.

- As far back as 1883, there were reports of Villa and Albion supporters clashing at Perry Barr before a game at Wellington Road, and two years later one of the most serious instances of Victorian football violence took place after a friendly with Preston, who won 5–1. The Preston team were surrounded by some of Villa's less sporting followers as they left the pitch and scuffles broke out. Players from both sides made their way to the tent which then acted as the dressing room and, according to the weekly paper *Saturday Night*, when they attempted to leave the ground some time later found the gates closed and a group of up to 2,000 'bona-fide Brummagem roughs' surrounding them and following their horse-drawn carriage for half a mile.
- Then, in January 1888, the cavalry were called to Perry Barr to deal with the crowd at an FA Cup tie, again with Preston, when the pitch was invaded on several occasions. This time, though, the crowd problems were down to overcrowding rather than violent intent on the part of the spectators.
- Nine years later, the opening game at Villa Park in 1897 was marred when Jabez Jackson, a local painter, stabbed a fellow spectator, Thomas Hodges, in the face with a pocket knife and was beaten by onlookers before being arrested and charged.
- A game against Brentford during September 1938 saw a spectator attempt to strike a visiting player. Four policemen

were needed to detain the fan, who was later barred from Villa Park for the remainder of the season, with the club ordered by the FA to post warning notices around the ground.

- Two months later, a Birmingham Combination game with Darlaston at the Alexandra Stadium in Perry Barr, where Villa's minor teams would often play their home games, had to be abandoned due to a pitch invasion. Quite why the crowd at such a low-key game, which would presumably only be numbered in the hundreds, would behave in such a way has never been explained.
- After the war it was reported that Villa fans taunted survivors of the Munich air crash when Manchester United were the visitors, while in 1967 Villa supporters were blamed for wrecking a train following a cup tie with Preston. In the same year, walking sticks were banned from Villa Park after incidents at a pre-season friendly with Blackburn Rovers. Hooliganism had started to become a serious matter.

— BOTTOM OF THE POPS —

In 2000, record label Cherry Red released a CD entitled *Come On You Villa* (CDGAFFER9). A few of the featured tracks were by respected musicians (such as post-punk icon and Villa supporter Spizz, plus Hurricane Smith, whose 'Theme From An Unmade Silent Movie' has been played at Villa Park for many years). The rest of the album, however, featured some of the worst musical atrocities ever to escape from a recording studio. For those with a macabre interest in such matters, the full track listing was:

A.S.T.O.N. V.I.L.L.A. – Dave Ismay and The Holte End
Come All You Villa – Loyal Band
We're Going Up – Aston Villa FC
Clarey Blue – Roy Green
We're The Holte End – Dave Ismay and The Holte End
Theme From An Unmade Silent Movie – Hurricane Smith
Villa Rock – Loyal Band
Holte End Hotel – Stephen Duffy

I Wanna Be There – Villa Sound
The Sun Never Sets On Aston Villa – Spizz Energi
Aston Villa (Claret And Blue) – David James and The Villa Squad
Villa Villa Come On – In Off The Bar
Let It Happen Now – V4 Villa
Ain't No Bluff – Villa Squad
Villa Oh Villa – Mark Adams

— TESTIMONIALS —

The following teams have provided the opposition in testimonial games for ex-Villa players:

Charlie Aitken: Coventry City (1969), Midlands Select (1977)
Michael Wright: Stoke City (1975)
Fred Turnbull: West Bromwich Albion (1976)
Keith Leonard: Villa 1974/75 (1978)
John Robson: International XI (1978)
Ron Saunders: Birmingham City (1980)
Brian Little: England (1982)
Dennis Mortimer: England (1985)
Nigel Spink: Wolves (1988)
Allan Evans: Walsall (1989)
Paul Birch: Wolves (1991)
Jimmy Dugdale: Birmingham City (1992)
Gordon Cowans: Stoke City (1993)
Paul McGrath: Birmingham City (1995)

— BEST MATES —

Villa have plenty of celebrity supporters, but they haven't always been limited to two legs. Best Mate was one of the most famous National Hunt jumpers of all time, winning the Cheltenham Gold Cup on three occasions. His owner, Jim Lewis, was a Villa fanatic whose racing colours are modelled on the 1957 FA Cup final strip and is reported to insist that all his guests on racedays wear claret-and-blue scarves. After Best Mate's third Cheltenham win, his owner paraded the Gold Cup on the pitch at Villa Park, during half-time of a Premier League game.

— THE HOLTE'S LAST STAND —

May 7th 1994, Aston Villa v Liverpool. Not only was it the final game of the season, it was also the last match to take place at Villa Park before the Holte End was demolished.

A crowd of 45,347, then a Premier League record, were in attendance with 19,210 of them standing on the Holte for the last time. Everyone entering the end was given a certificate stating 'I WAS THERE'. The club had attempted to get together every former Villa player who had ever scored at that end of the ground, and most of them were on the pitch before the game. All was set for a celebration of the biggest and the best terrace in football. Enter Dave Chance . . .

Dave worked for the Villa as a matchday compere, entertaining the corporate guests and doing some pitchside announcing, so he was a natural to lead a bit of community singing before kick-off. Unfortunately, the song Dave was asked to sing was *You'll Never Walk Alone*. And Villa, remember, were playing Liverpool. Oh dear.

Dave, resplendent for some reason in a pink suit, got as far as midway through the first line without incident. Then the crowd began to react. Boos, jeers, whistles, abuse. Dave struggled manfully on to the end of the song then left the pitch, his face the same colour as his suit. Whatever the song may have said, Dave certainly did walk alone.

The team attempted to further ruin the occasion by going a goal down, but two second-half goals from Dwight Yorke gave the Holte End a fitting send-off and everyone was happy.

As the crowd dispersed, some supporters took more permanent souvenirs home with them. Signs, barriers and even toilet fittings were torn down and last seen headed away from Villa Park. Some, though, attempted to take things too far, as the PA announcement demonstrated: "Would the people trying to remove the Trinity Road gates please leave them where they are. We're not demolishing that one."

As the Holte finally emptied, one group wrenched off the sign which stated "NO AWAY SUPPORTERS AT THIS END" from the outside wall and carried it away, just as the coaches of Liverpool fans were driving down Witton Lane. With the shared bond that links all football supporters, they applauded the looters as both began their journeys home.

— GREAT VILLANS: GRAHAM TAYLOR —

Taylor spent his injury-shortened playing career in the lower divisions before becoming, at the age of 28, one of the youngest managers in league history when he took over at Lincoln City. Here he won the Fourth Division title with a record points haul before performing miracles at Watford, who he took from the Fourth Division to runners-up in the First together with an FA Cup final appearance. Taylor also oversaw Watford's pioneering work in the community.

In the summer of 1987 Taylor felt that the time was right for a fresh challenge and moved to newly-relegated Villa, who he initially described as "a shambles." He got rid of several big names, replacing them with journeymen whose job was to get Villa back to the First Division. This was achieved on the final day of the season, with the aid of Taylor's first transfer masterstroke, David Platt, signed from Crewe for £200,000.

1988/89 saw Villa get off to a good start in the top flight, thanks mainly to a scoring spree from Alan McInally, bought from Celtic the previous year. However, once McInally's goals dried up the team slid down the table and were only saved from relegation by a point. During this season, Villa went on a tour of Trinidad and Tobago, where Taylor spotted and signed Dwight Yorke.

The summer of 1989 saw Taylor complete his third great signing, when persuading Doug Ellis to smash the club's rigid pay structure and buy Paul McGrath from Manchester United. After a rocky start, Villa ended 1989/90 in runners-up spot, which was enough to earn them a place in the following season's UEFA Cup.

Taylor then left to take the England job. His failings here have been well-documented, partly because his managerial style was not suited to the international stage, but also due to injuries to key players and the dearth of quality available for selection. He then returned to club management with Wolves, where he was one of many managers who failed to gain promotion, and later moved back to Watford. Here Taylor performed another miracle, taking them from Division Two to the Premier League before resigning as manager at the end of 2000/01.

Taylor was then appointed a non-executive director of Villa, insisting he had no intention of returning to management. However, the resignation of John Gregory in February 2002 led to Taylor's return as Villa manager. There was no happy reunion – in many ways the modern game had passed him by and he struggled to cope with the in-fighting and factionalism that was beginning to dog the club.

Taylor resigned at the end of the 2002/03 season, when Villa narrowly avoided relegation. His return had been an unsuccessful one, but his first spell ensures his place in Villa Park legend. He may never have won any trophies, but Graham Taylor reversed a decline that many believed to be terminal, signed three of the club's greatest modern-day players and his work gave future managers a platform on which to build success.

— GREAT GAMES 8: THE ONE-SIDED FINAL —

Villa 3 **Leeds United 0**
Milosevic
Taylor
Yorke

March 24th 1996: Coca-Cola Cup final
Wembley
Att: 77,065

In 1994 Villa supporters had attended the final of this competition determined to enjoy the occasion against Manchester United, but with little expectation of the success that came courtesy of Ron Atkinson's tactics. Two years later, they arrived at Wembley as though they belonged there, confident of adding another League Cup to the club's roll of honour.

Leeds manager Howard Wilkinson helped the Villa's cause with a bizarre team selection – he would end the afternoon being booed by his own supporters – but whoever he picked would have been unable to live with Brian Little's players.

Some of the club's greatest achievements have come against the odds, but here was a Villa side once more striding the big stage as though it was theirs by right. With Mark Draper and captain Andy Townsend controlling midfield from the first whistle the team had already missed a couple of chances before the much-maligned Savo Milosevic opened the scoring with a 25-yard screamer after 20 minutes. They had several more opportunities before Ian Taylor, who had watched the final with United from a vantage point alongside the rest of the Villa supporters, scored Villa's second ten minutes after the re-start with a shot from the edge of the penalty area.

The game was won by this point and Villa could relax in the almost certainty that the cup was won. Wing-backs Gary Charles and Alan Wright pushed forward regularly while Paul McGrath had rarely enjoyed an easier game.

Dwight Yorke got a third a minute from time following strong work from Milosevic and saw an injury-time shot fly inches wide, but Villa had one of the most one-sided finals Wembley has ever witnessed won well before then. As an added bonus, as Andy Townsend went up to receive the trophy (bizarrely from Health Minister Virginia Bottomley), the figure of West Bromwich

Albion chairman Bert Millichip looked on, appearing distinctly unimpressed at the sight of his club's old rivals adding yet another trophy to their collection.

This was Villa's fifth League Cup win, which equalled Liverpool's record of the time (although the Reds have since pulled ahead, with two further successes). Watching the confident, almost arrogant, way in which Little's side strolled around Wembley, the general feeling was that it would be the first of many triumphs for him and his promising young team. However, as has been the case too often with Villa in recent times, what seemed like the beginning of a successful era was also its high point and 11 years on, the 1996 Coca-Cola Cup remains Villa's last trophy to date.

— AND IT'S CALTHORPE VILLA . . . —

The most powerful football club in the city at the time of Villa's formation was Calthorpe FC, who had earlier changed their name from Birmingham Clerks FC. However, Calthorpe moved to a ground on Bristol Road, close to what is now the Birmingham University campus, and as a condition of their tenancy could not charge for admission. As payments to players became more commonplace (even before professionalism was legalised in 1885) Calthorpe found themselves unable to match the spending of such newcomers as Villa and West Bromwich Albion.

Yet their fame was such that they could still have remained the major force in Birmingham football had not Archie Hunter, new to the city after arriving from his native Ayr, been unable to find his way to their ground. Hunter instead chose to join his fellow-Scot George Ramsay in Aston and became the first great Villa player, captaining the club to their FA Cup triumph of 1887.

— BACK IN EUROPE —

Villa were the first English team to play in Europe after the five-year ban imposed by UEFA after the Hysel stadium tragedy was lifted. The UEFA Cup game at home to Czech club Banik Ostrava on September 19th 1990 kicked off 15 minutes before Manchester United's European Cup Winners' Cup tie with Hungarian outfit Pesci Munkas.

— CLUB SCAPEGOATS —

Every club has one – the player who fans reckon can't do anything right. Here are a few who have taken the role at Villa Park over the years.

Tony Hateley (1963–66): 86 goals in 148 games is a record to be proud of at any level, let alone while playing for a perennially-struggling First Division side. Yet for some reason Hateley regularly got stick from the Villa Park crowd. "If he scored from thirty yards they moaned that it wasn't from forty. If he scored a twice they complained he hadn't got a hat-trick," was the comment from one mystified supporter. Maybe it was because when Hateley was signed from Notts County supporters retained fond memories of the popular Gerry Hitchens, but he was never fully accepted by the crowd and later moved to Chelsea.

John Robson (1972–79): Signed from Derby County, Robson was a midfielder-cum-full-back who found the task of replacing Charlie Aitken a difficult one and was generally held to be personally responsible every time the team lost, even when he wasn't playing. Supporters' feelings towards Robson mellowed during the successful 1976/77 season, but the following year he tragically contracted multiple sclerosis and was later forced to retire. He died of the disease in 2004.

Ken McNaught (1977–83): Yet another player who found the task of replacing a popular figure, in this case Chris Nicholl, to be fraught with difficulty. McNaught gradually won the crowd round, but forever seemed to be at the heart of disappointments – giving away a penalty in the FA Cup quarter-final of 1980 and being responsible for conceding a vital goal against Ipswich the following season were just two of the charges levelled against him. History has rightly been kind to McNaught and he is now regarded as an unsung hero of the European Cup-winning side, but at the time he was definitely club scapegoat.

Bernie Gallagher (1985–91): A regular throughout the Second Division promotion season and a squad player for some time afterwards, Gallagher may not have been the most talented Villa player of all time but he didn't deserve the derision he received while at the club.

Peter Crouch (2002–03): Signed by Graham Taylor and 6′ 7″, both of which were crimes in the eyes of some Villa supporters of the time. Crouch started off his Villa career well enough, but a couple of missed chances saw him abused by sections of the crowd and he was dropped from the first team, never again to figure in the plans of either Taylor or his successor, David O'Leary. Loaned out to Norwich then sold to Southampton before a big-money move to Liverpool and a regular England place, Crouch's subsequent career became an embarrassment both to O'Leary and, one hopes, those who booed him at Villa.

Lee Hendrie (1995–2007): More of an anti-hero than a scapegoat, but Hendrie's rumoured allegiance to Birmingham City Football Club meant he could always be relied upon to take any blame that was going throughout his colourful and ultimately disappointing Villa career.

— CHAMPIONS VII: 1980/81 —

Seventy-one years after their sixth championship, Villa finally earned a seventh. They used just 14 players in the 42-game season and, although generally ignored and unfancied throughout the campaign, won the title by four points as runners-up Ipswich collapsed in the final stages.

	P	W	D	L	F	A	Pts
Aston Villa	**42**	**26**	**8**	**8**	**72**	**40**	**60**
Ipswich Town	42	23	10	9	77	43	56
Arsenal	42	19	15	8	61	45	53
West Bromwich Albion	42	20	12	10	60	42	52
Liverpool	42	17	17	8	62	42	51
Southampton	42	20	10	12	76	56	50
Nottingham Forest	42	19	12	11	62	44	50
Manchester United	42	15	18	9	51	36	48
Leeds United	42	17	10	15	39	47	44
Tottenham Hotspur	42	14	15	13	70	68	43
Stoke City	42	12	18	12	51	60	42
Manchester City	42	14	11	17	56	59	39
Birmingham City	42	13	12	17	50	61	38
Middlesbrough	42	16	5	21	53	61	37
Everton	42	13	10	19	55	58	36
Coventry City	42	13	10	19	48	68	36
Sunderland	42	14	7	21	52	53	35
Wolverhampton Wanderers	42	13	9	20	43	55	35
Brighton & Hove Albion	42	14	7	21	54	67	35
Norwich City	42	13	7	22	49	73	33
Leicester City	42	13	6	23	40	67	32
Crystal Palace	42	6	7	29	47	83	19

— GREAT VILLANS: GORDON COWANS —

Gordon Cowans: A Villa career of triumph and tragedy

In February 1976 a 17 year-old midfielder made his Villa debut, as substitute in a 2–1 defeat away at Manchester City. The following season saw him become established in the first team, gaining a League Cup winners medal after taking part in the marathon final against Everton, while a broken leg suffered by Alex Cropley in December 1977 meant that he was now a first-choice in the Villa midfield.

Gordon Sidney Cowans went on to play 531 times for the Villa (the third highest-number in the club's history) during a career which saw him leave three times only to return on each occasion, twice as a player and the final time to take joint charge of the club's Academy, a position he still holds.

Cowans was an ever-present in the Villa side for four consecutive seasons between 1979 and 1983 as the team set about conquering Europe, winning the Robinson's Barley Water Young

Player of the Year award for 1979/80 and captaining the England under-21s along the way. In February 1983 he made his international debut, playing for England against Wales. Cowans was now widely regarded as the best playmaker in the league, but tragedy struck when he suffered a broken leg during a tournament in Barcelona prior to the 1983/84 season. Coming just weeks before the injury which was to ruin Gary Shaw's career, this double setback was a blow from which the Villa side of that era never recovered.

Cowans made his way back into the first team for 1984/85, by which time manager Tony Barton had been replaced by Graham Turner, but the summer of 1985 saw Gordon and team-mate Paul Rideout transferred to Serie A side Bari for a combined fee of £800,000.

Gordon suffered further serious injury and his team were relegated in his first year. However, he regained much of his previous form, winning back his place in the England side although Bari were unable to return to the top division of Italian football. In the summer of 1988 Cowans retuned to Villa, newly-promoted under Graham Taylor. When Taylor became England manager he found room for Gordon in his team for a European Championship game against the Republic of Ireland. This was Cowans' tenth cap, and he was never on the losing side.

In 1991 Ron Atkinson sold Cowans for £200,000 to Blackburn (inspiring the title of the Villa fanzine *Missing Sid*), where the player spent two years witnessing the spending spree financed by steel magnate Jack Walker.

— INTERNATIONAL DUTY —

Villa have supplied full internationals for 24 countries. Apart from the home nations there have been claret and blue caps for Australia, Bulgaria, Cameroon, Colombia, Croatia, the Czech Republic, Denmark, Ecuador, Germany, Ghana, Israel, Morocco, the Netherlands, Norway, Peru, Poland, the Republic of Ireland, Sweden, Turkey and Yugoslavia.

— GREAT GAMES 9: THE MATCH THAT WON THE LEAGUE —

Aston Villa 2 **Liverpool 0**
Withe
Mortimer

January 11th 1981: Division One
Villa Park
Att: 47,960

Titles are won over the course of a season. Maybe, but one match can often play a massive part in deciding the result of a title race that ends several months later.

On 11th January 1981 Liverpool were top of the table on goal difference from Villa in second place. Having gone out of the FA Cup to Ipswich the previous week, and with their title chances roundly belittled by all and sundry, Villa needed a big performance. In every way, they gave one.

Villa began brightly, with Tony Morley and Gary Shaw causing problems for the Liverpool defence. In contrast, any attacking threat the visitors presented was easily contained by central defenders Ken McNaught and Allan Evans. With 19 minutes gone, Villa went ahead with a goal that was becoming their trademark. Morley beat Liverpool full-back Richard Money, got to the bye-line and sent over a low cross met on the turn by Shaw. His shot was parried by Liverpool keeper Ray Clemence and the ball fell to Peter Withe, who stabbed home to give his side a deserved lead.

Villa had several more chances during the first half, but after the restart spent long periods on the defensive as Liverpool began looking more like the side that was to win that season's European Cup. Villa's defending became increasingly desperate and watching Scotland national manager Jock Stein could not fail to have been impressed by the way his countrymen McNaught and Evans performed under pressure.

Then, with eight minutes to go, came the incident everyone present will long remember. Des Bremner won the ball and passed to Kenny Swain, who ran forty yards before passing to Shaw. A casual back-heel from the Villa forward set free Dennis Mortimer, whose trademark surging run took him to the edge of the Liverpool area and past Clemence as he pushed the ball into the empty Holte End net.

There may have still been 16 games to go, but as far as Villa supporters were concerned this was the turning point. From the second Mortimer's goal hit the back of the net their team were destined to win the championship.

Given a free transfer at the end of the 1992/93 season, Cowans returned to Villa Park and played 11 games before leaving once more, headed for Derby County. Spells with Wolves, Sheffield United, Bradford City, Stockport County and Burnley then ensued before he finally hung up his boots in 1997, after playing almost a 1,000 first-class matches.

It was no surprise when Gordon returned to Villa for a fourth spell, as youth coach. This unprecedented fourth spell at Villa Park has seen the FA Youth Cup won in 2002 and players such as Gabriel Agbonlahor, Luke Moore and Gary Cahill rising through the ranks to become first team regulars. In 2010 Gordon became first-team coach.

Despite losing potentially his best years to injury and then the lower reaches of Italian football, Cowans remains one of the all-time Villa Park greats. David Platt was once asked his biggest footballing ambition. "To make a run Gordon Cowans doesn't spot," was the reply.

— LONG SERVICE 2 —

The retirement of Villa secretary Steve Stride in the summer of 2007 brought to an end one of the most incredible dynasties in world football. Stride was only the fifth man to hold the position in a period dating back nearly 130 years almost to the very beginning of the club.

George Ramsay (see *Great Villans: George Ramsay*, page 12) became the first Villa secretary in 1884, holding the post until his retirement in 1926. He was then succeeded by Billy Smith, who remained in the role until 1955, handing over to his long-serving assistant Fred Archer.

Archer was Villa secretary until 1968, and his successor, Alan Bennett, came from Leicester City, which meant that he was the only man appointed from outside the club to do the job.

Bennett lasted a 'mere' 12 years before his assistant, Steve Stride, took over in 1980. For one job to have been performed by just five men since 1886 is a major achievement in any walk of life. In the fast-moving world of football it verges on the miraculous.

— INFLATION —

In Villa's double-winning season of 1896/97, the club's accounts revealed an income of £109,986, of which gate receipts made up £10,192. Wage and transfer fees accounted for £3,999 of expenses and there was a total profit of £1,299. In 2010/11, when the club finished ninth in the Premier League, turnover had increased to a record £92 million, of which £21.45 million was match-day income. However, expenditure had grown by so much that the club still recorded a loss of £53.9 million.

— AND MY FAVOURITES —

The author's all-time Villa XI, based on players seen and not including current ones, is as follows:

Jimmy Rimmer (1977–83; 287 games)
John Gidman (1972–79; 242 games, 9 goals)
Colin Gibson (1978–85; 233 games, 17 goals)
Allan Evans (1977–89; 466 games, 62 goals)
Paul McGrath (1989–96; 315 games, 9 goals)
Dennis Mortimer (1975–85; 405 games, 36 goals)
Tony Morley (1979–83; 170 games, 34 goals)
Brian Little (1970–82; 306 games, 82 goals)
Peter Withe (1980–85; 232 games 92 goals)
Gordon Cowans (1976–85, 88-91, 93–94; 531 games, 59 goals)
David Platt (1988–91; 145 games, 68 goals)

— YOUR STARTERS FOR TEN —

Who was the first British player to be awarded a Champions League winners medal? Who, for that matter, was the first British player to win Europe's premier club honour while playing for an overseas side? As every keen pub quizzer and all Villa supporters will know, the answer to both questions is, of course, Paul Lambert, who was in the Borussia Dortmund team which beat Juventus in the 1997 final.

Paul had already tasted playing success with St Mirren, where he won the Scottish Cup, and Motherwell, where he finished runners-up in the Scottish Premier League under future Villa boss Alex McLeish. He then spent a season with Dortmund before moving to Celtic, with whom he won four Scottish league titles, three Scottish FA Cups and two Scottish League Cups. Paul played 40 times for Scotland and was later inducted into the Scottish Football Hall of Fame, in 2009. After an undistinguished start to his managerial career, notably with Wycombe and Colchester, Paul created another record when he became the first manager to win League One and the Championship in successive seasons, while manager of Norwich City.

Although the Scottish influence at Villa Park has long been established, this has mainly been confined to the playing and administration sides of the club, with Villa's six previous managers from north of the border having failed to win a single honour between them. It is to be hoped that this unenviable record will soon be broken.

— THE FINAL WORD —

"The door to the lavishly-appointed Guest Room at Villa Park was open and out in the corridor the little boys, dodging the commissionaire, were calling for Brian Little and John Gidman. Quite rightly, they took no notice of myself and the elderly bald-headed man, bespectacled, stooping a little, who was quietly finishing his tea. He looked at them for a moment, a whimsical look, and moved to the long windows overlooking the now deserted playing pitch.

Every time you come here it must bring back memories, Pongo' I said. He stared out for a long while. I thought he'd forgotten I was there. 'Aye,' he said suddenly 'aye, they're a great club . . . the greatest.' I stood and looked with him, this old man whose goals had set the Villa crowds roaring so long ago. It was not quite dusk on that March afternoon and I saw them too . . . they were out again, the old ghosts . . . Jack Hughes, scorer just about one hundred years earlier of Aston Villa's first goal (perhaps to the very day) . . . George Ramsay . . . the Hunter brothers . . . Willie McGregor . . . Denny Hodgetts . . . legion upon legion of them on parade now, filling the field with claret and blue . . . the century with pride."

Taken from *Aston Villa – The First 100 Years*, by Peter Morris.

— VILLA'S SEASON-BY-SEASON RECORD —

Season	Div	P	W	D	L	F	A	W	D	L	F	A	Pts	Pos
1888/89	1	22	10	0	1	44	16	2	5	4	17	27	29	2nd
1889/90	1	22	6	2	3	30	15	1	3	7	13	36	19	8th
1890/91	1	22	5	4	2	29	18	2	0	9	16	40	18	9th
1891/92	1	26	10	0	3	63	23	5	0	8	26	33	33	4th
1892/93	1	30	12	1	2	50	24	4	2	9	23	38	35	4th
1893/94	1	30	12	2	1	49	13	7	4	4	35	29	44	1st
1894/95	1	30	12	2	1	51	12	5	3	7	31	31	39	3rd
1895/96	1	30	14	1	0	47	17	6	4	5	31	28	45	1st
1896/97	1	30	10	3	2	36	16	11	2	2	37	22	47	1st
1897/98	1	30	12	1	2	47	21	2	4	9	14	30	33	6th
1898/99	1	34	15	2	0	58	13	4	5	8	18	27	45	1st
1899/00	1	34	12	4	1	45	18	10	2	5	32	17	50	1st
1900/01	1	34	8	5	4	32	18	2	5	10	13	33	30	15th
1901/02	1	34	9	5	3	27	13	4	3	10	15	27	34	8th
1902/03	1	34	11	3	3	43	18	8	0	9	18	22	41	2nd
1903/04	1	34	13	1	3	41	16	4	6	7	29	32	41	5th
1904/05	1	34	11	2	4	32	15	8	2	7	31	28	42	4th
1905/06	1	38	13	2	4	51	19	4	4	11	21	37	40	8th
1906/07	1	38	13	4	2	51	19	6	2	11	27	33	44	5th
1907/08	1	38	9	6	4	47	24	8	3	8	30	35	43	2nd
1908/09	1	38	8	7	4	31	22	6	3	10	27	34	38	7th
1909/10	1	38	17	2	0	62	19	6	5	8	22	23	53	1st
1910/11	1	38	15	3	1	50	18	7	4	8	19	23	51	2nd
1911/12	1	38	12	2	5	48	22	5	5	9	28	41	41	6th
1912/13	1	38	13	4	2	57	21	6	8	5	29	31	50	2nd
1913/14	1	38	11	3	5	36	21	8	3	8	29	29	44	2nd
1914/15	1	38	10	5	4	39	32	3	6	10	23	40	37	14th
First World War														
1919/20	1	42	11	3	7	49	36	7	3	11	26	37	42	9th
1920/21	1	42	11	4	6	39	21	7	3	11	24	49	43	10th
1921/22	1	42	16	3	2	50	19	6	0	15	24	36	47	5th
1922/23	1	42	15	3	3	42	11	3	7	11	22	40	46	6th
1923/24	1	42	10	10	1	33	11	8	3	10	19	26	49	6th

1924/25	1	42	10	7	4	34	25	3	6	12	24	46	39	15th
1925/26	1	42	12	7	2	56	25	4	5	12	30	51	44	6th
1926/27	1	42	11	4	6	51	34	7	3	11	30	49	43	10th
1927/28	1	42	13	3	5	52	30	4	6	11	26	43	43	8th
1928/29	1	42	16	2	3	62	30	7	2	12	36	51	50	3rd
1929/30	1	42	13	1	7	54	33	8	4	9	38	50	47	4th
1929/31	1	42	17	3	1	86	34	8	6	7	42	44	59	2nd
1931/32	1	42	15	1	5	64	28	4	7	10	40	44	46	5th
1932/33	1	42	16	2	3	60	29	7	6	8	32	38	54	2nd
1933/34	1	42	10	5	6	45	34	4	7	10	33	41	40	13th
1934/35	1	42	11	6	4	50	36	3	7	11	24	52	41	13th
1935/36	1	42	7	6	8	47	56	6	3	12	34	54	35	21st*
1936/37	2	42	10	6	5	47	30	6	6	9	35	40	44	9th
1937/38	2	42	17	2	2	50	12	8	5	8	23	23	57	1st*
1938/39	1	42	11	3	7	44	25	5	6	10	27	35	41	12th
1939/40	1	3	1	1	0	3	1	0	0	1	0	1	1	10th
(Season abandoned due to the outbreak of war)														
Second World War														
1946/47	1	42	9	6	6	39	24	9	3	9	28	29	45	8th
1947/48	1	42	13	5	3	42	22	6	4	11	23	35	47	6th
1948/49	1	42	10	6	5	40	36	6	4	11	20	40	42	10th
1949/50	1	42	10	7	4	31	19	5	5	11	30	42	42	12th
1950/51	1	42	9	6	6	39	29	3	7	11	27	39	37	15th
1951/52	1	42	13	3	5	49	28	6	6	9	30	42	47	6th
1952/53	1	42	9	7	5	36	23	5	6	10	27	38	41	11th
1953/54	1	42	12	5	4	50	28	4	4	13	20	40	41	13th
1954/55	1	42	11	3	7	38	31	9	4	8	34	42	47	6th
1955/56	1	42	9	6	6	32	29	2	7	12	20	40	35	20th
1956/57	1	42	10	8	3	45	25	4	7	10	20	30	43	10th
1957/58	1	42	12	4	5	46	26	4	3	14	27	60	39	14th
1958/59	1	42	8	5	8	31	33	3	3	15	27	54	30	21st+
1959/60	2	42	17	3	1	62	19	8	6	7	27	24	59	1st*
1960/61	1	42	13	3	5	48	28	4	6	11	30	49	43	9th
1961/62	1	42	13	5	3	45	20	5	3	13	20	36	44	7th
1962/63	1	42	12	2	7	38	23	3	6	12	24	45	38	15th
1963/64	1	42	8	6	7	35	29	3	6	12	27	42	34	19th

1964/65	1	42	14	1	6	36	24	2	4	15	21	58	37	16th
1965/66	1	42	10	3	8	39	34	5	3	13	30	46	36	16th
1966/67	1	42	7	5	9	30	33	4	2	15	24	52	29	21st+
1967/68	2	42	10	3	8	35	30	5	4	12	19	34	37	16th
1968/69	2	42	10	8	3	22	11	2	6	13	15	37	38	18th
1969/70	2	42	7	8	6	23	21	1	5	15	13	41	29	21st+
1970/71	3	46	13	7	3	27	13	6	8	9	27	33	53	4th
1971/72	3	46	20	1	2	45	10	12	5	6	40	22	70	1st*
1972/73	2	42	12	5	4	27	17	6	9	6	24	30	50	3rd
1973/74	2	42	8	9	4	33	21	5	6	10	15	24	41	14th
1974/75	2	42	16	4	1	47	6	9	4	8	32	26	58	2nd*
1975/76	1	42	11	8	2	32	17	0	9	12	19	42	39	16th
1976/77	1	42	17	3	1	55	17	5	4	12	21	33	51	4th
1977/78	1	42	11	4	6	33	18	7	6	8	24	24	46	8th
1978/79	1	42	8	9	4	37	26	7	7	7	22	23	46	8th
1979/80	1	42	11	5	5	29	22	5	9	7	22	28	46	7th
1980/81	1	42	16	3	2	40	13	10	5	6	32	27	60	1st
1981/82	1	42	9	6	6	28	24	6	6	9	27	29	57*	11th
1982/83	1	42	17	2	2	47	15	4	3	14	15	35	68	6th
1983/84	1	42	14	3	4	34	22	3	6	12	25	39	60	10th
1984/85	1	42	10	7	4	34	20	5	4	12	26	40	56	10th
1985/86	1	42	7	6	8	27	28	3	8	10	24	39	44	16th
1986/87	1	42	7	7	7	25	25	1	5	15	20	54	36	22nd+
1987/88	2	44	9	7	6	31	21	13	5	4	37	20	78	2nd*
1988/89	1	38	7	6	6	25	22	2	7	10	20	34	40	17th
1989/90	1	38	13	3	3	36	20	8	4	7	21	18	70	2nd
1990/91	1	38	7	9	3	29	25	2	5	12	17	33	41	17th
1991/92	1	42	13	3	5	31	16	4	6	11	17	28	60	7th
1992/93	Prem	42	13	5	3	36	16	8	6	7	21	24	74	2nd
1993/94	Prem	42	8	5	8	23	18	7	7	7	23	32	57	10th
1994/95	Prem	42	6	9	6	27	24	5	6	10	24	32	48	18th
1995/96	Prem	38	11	5	3	32	15	7	4	8	20	20	63	4th
1996/97	Prem	38	11	5	3	27	13	6	5	8	20	21	61	5th
1997/98	Prem	38	9	3	7	26	24	8	3	8	23	24	57	7th
1998/99	Prem	38	10	3	6	33	28	5	7	7	18	18	55	6th
1999/00	Prem	38	8	8	3	23	12	7	5	7	23	23	58	6th

2000/01	Prem	38	8	8	3	27	20	5	7	7	19	23	54	8th
2000/02	Prem	38	8	7	4	22	17	4	7	8	24	30	50	8th
2002/03	Prem	38	11	2	6	25	14	1	7	11	17	33	45	16th
2003/04	Prem	38	9	6	4	24	19	6	5	8	24	25	56	6th
2004/05	Prem	38	8	6	5	26	17	4	5	10	19	35	47	10th
2005/06	Prem	38	6	6	7	20	20	4	6	9	22	35	42	16th
2006/07	Prem	38	7	8	4	20	14	4	9	6	23	27	50	11th
2007/08	Prem	38	10	3	6	34	22	6	9	4	37	29	60	6th
2008/09	Prem	38	7	9	3	27	21	10	2	7	27	27	62	6th
2009/10	Prem	38	8	8	3	29	16	9	5	5	23	23	64	6th
2010/11	Prem	38	8	7	4	26	19	4	5	10	22	40	48	9th
2011/12	Prem	38	4	7	8	20	25	3	10	6	17	28	38	16th

* relegated
+ Promoted
^ Three points for a win introduced

Selected Bibliography

Aston Villa – The First 100 Years, Peter Morris (Naldrett Press)

Pinnacle of the Perry Barr Pets, Simon Page (Juma)

Illustrated History of Aston Villa 1874–1988, Graham McColl (Hamlyn)

The Football Grounds of Great Britain, Simon Inglis (Willow)

Soccer History Issue 10, Ian Nannestad (Soccer History Ltd)

Villa Park 100 Years, Simon Inglis (Sports Projects)

Kicking & Screaming, Rogan Taylor (Robson Books)

Road to Rotterdam, Rob Bishop (Brite Spot)

Children of the Revolution, Richard Whitehead (Sports Projects)

The Villans, a Day to Day Life, Graham Betts (Mainstream)